Frontispiece:

The Bat
Dish, 10⅜ in. long, c. 1785
(Dyson Perrins Museum)

WORCESTER BLUE AND WHITE PORCELAIN
1751–1790

AN ILLUSTRATED ENCYCLOPAEDIA OF THE PATTERNS

Lawrence Branyan,
Neal French
and John Sandon

Barrie & Jenkins
London Melbourne Sydney Auckland Johannesburg

Eastview Editions, Inc.
Westfield, N.J.

Barrie & Jenkins Ltd

An imprint of the Hutchinson Publishing Group

3 Fitzroy Square, London W1P 6JD

Hutchinson Group (Australia) Pty Ltd
30–32 Cremorne Street, Richmond South, Victoria 3121
PO Box 151, Broadway, New South Wales 2007

Hutchinson Group (NZ) Ltd
32–34 View Road, PO Box 40–086, Glenfield, Auckland 10

Hutchinson Group (SA) (Pty) Ltd
PO Box 337, Bergvlei 2012, South Africa

First published 1981
© Dyson Perrins Museum Trust 1981

Published in the United States of America in 1981 by
Eastview Editions, Inc.
P.O. Box 783
Westfield, N.J. 07091

Set in Monophoto Ehrhardt

Filmset and printed in Great Britain by BAS Printers, Over Wallop, Hants
and bound by Wm Brendon and Son Ltd, Tiptree, Essex

Contents

Preface

This book is about Worcester porcelain, or more specifically, about the wares made at that factory which were decorated with cobalt oxides prior to the application of the glaze, and are therefore referred to as 'underglaze blue' or 'blue and white' porcelains. We have concentrated primarily upon the patterns which were used to decorate these wares, both the painted designs as in the earlier production of the factory, and the transfer-printed decoration which prevailed in the later years. The book covers a period which begins in the early 1750s, when 'The Worcester Tonquin Manufacture' was begun by Dr John Wall and his partners, and ends around 1790, by which time the market demand for underglaze blue wares had so diminished that their manufacture became a much less significant part of total production.

It has only been in comparatively recent years that any widespread attention has been given by porcelain dealers and collectors to the blue and white products made by the Worcester factory and its English competitors during the eighteenth century. Indeed, the great Worcester collections built up in the Victorian era and in the earlier years of this century, and the magnificent books illustrating the Worcester wares of the so-called 'First Period' were, to an overwhelming extent, concentrated on the polychrome-enamelled onglaze products of the Warmstry House factory. While one must surely give due regard to these beautifully made and colourful wares, and recognize their historic and artistic contribution to the English heritage, it still must be remembered that the blue and white porcelain was the 'bread and butter' of the Worcester factory, constituting what must have been well over 75 per cent of its total output during these first forty years of existence. Blue and white porcelain was the everyday tableware of the moderately well-to-do English family of that day; it was never inexpensive, even by today's standards, but it was durable, attractive, and eminently suitable for the purpose intended.

Perhaps it was because of these very qualities that the blue and white Worcester wares were somehow considered to be inferior to their polychrome-decorated counterparts, except in the eyes of those comparatively few perceptive collectors who recognized the quality which they embodied. Nevertheless, over the last two decades, Worcester blue and white has come to be thought of as one of the most vital and individual categories of porcelain in the world.

In 1969, when the first of what was to be a series of excavations – to which we refer throughout this book – had been completed on the original Warmstry House factory site at Worcester, the new curator of the Dyson Perrins Museum, Henry Sandon, came to believe that using the evidence from the excavations that would follow, it might just be possible to categorize the designs which had been used to decorate the blue and white porcelains into the form of a 'pattern book'. Such a book, he felt, could be of great importance and use to both dealers in, and collectors of, blue and white porcelain made at Worcester, particularly since the original factory pattern books had not survived. It was then that this book began. As our work has progressed over the years, there have been two apparently irreparable disappointments to those original expectations. Firstly, we have found that while the factory site excavations have produced evidence which was immensely useful, indeed essential, to our work, many if not most of the patterns of unmistakably Worcester origin could not be matched with exact duplicates found in the waste pits of Warmstry House. Therefore, our conclusions as to what was and was not a Worcester pattern could not in any way be based exclusively on factory site evidence. Secondly, we have had to confess failure in not including in this book *all* of the Worcester designs used to decorate the blue and white ware; we are quite certain that while we have located what must be a very large proportion of the patterns so used, there are many others that have not been included, either because we were unaware of their existence, or, in some fewer cases, because we have not been able to locate an example of the pattern which could be illustrated here.

There is no way in which one person or any group of persons could assemble a book of this nature without the assistance and encouragement of many others. And this we have received in great abundance from a wide range of dealers, collectors, museum and auction house staff who, in many cases, have gone to much trouble and even expense to lend us a helping hand. While it is really not possible to mention each of them, we surely must extend our appreciation to the Trustees of the Dyson Perrins Museum at Worcester, who gave us free access to that magnificent collection and allowed us to photograph so many of the rare and beautiful pieces which they own; to John Mallet and Michael Archer of the Victoria and Albert Museum, for photographs of the outstanding examples in that fine collection of English porcelains; to Hugh Tait and Mrs A. Dawson of the British Museum; Norma Watt of the Castle Museum, Norwich and Sheenah Smith who was formerly associated there; the staff of the Ashmolean Museum at Oxford; and the Trustees of the National Trust and staff of Trerice House,

Newquay, Cornwall, all for photographs so willingly supplied to us. We must also thank Sylvia Hunte and Joanna Forester of Sotheby Parke Bernet and Co. and Anton Gabczewicz of Christie, Manson and Wood for their assistance in locating and supplying needed illustrations from their catalogues.

Our particular appreciation must be expressed to that great authority, Geoffrey Godden of Worthing, who not only opened his own reference collection to us and gave us use of so many of his photographs of Worcester blue and white which he has compiled through the years, but also kindly consented to correct and comment upon the text of this book; to Simon Spero of China Choice Antiques, who, in addition to several photographs, most kindly provided valuable information about the patterns, and whose own enthusiasm for blue and white greatly encouraged us in the project; to Mrs Anne George of Albert Amor Ltd of London; to Miss Pamela Klaber of Klaber and Klaber Antiques; to Mrs Sheila Davis of Venner's Antiques; to Mrs Hoff of Hoff Antiques; to Mrs Cometa Warner of W. W. Warner (Antiques) Ltd of Brasted, Kent: and to Billy Buck of Steppes Hill Farm Antiques of Sittingbourne, Kent, each of whom made available so many of the photographs which we have used.

We must also warmly thank Tom Burn of Rous Lench, near Worcester, and Gilbert Bradley of London, both of whom graciously allowed us to borrow pieces from their splendid private collections to be photographed for the book, and made it possible for us to include illustrations of many of the rare patterns which would otherwise have been omitted.

Many of the private collectors who allowed us to photograph their choice pieces for inclusion in the book have not been mentioned here by name at their own request; and it is a sad commentary on the times in which we live that we must recognize their desire for anonymity. Nevertheless, they know themselves of the great contribution they have made to this book, and we extend to them all our heartfelt thanks.

The photographs which were not supplied to us by these generous people were taken by either

Chris Halton, who did the illustrations from our own collections and other private collections, or by John and Joan Beckerley, who photographed the majority of the pieces in the Dyson Perrins Museum collection. The quality of their work speaks for itself, and we were most fortunate to have had use of their skills.

We must not forget, too, Dick Reid and George Walker of Esso Europe Inc. Headquarters management in London, who for many years provided us with a roof over our heads as we worked on the book in the aftermath of the business day, and, as importantly, generously opened the company coffee machine to keep us going; Ted Tibbles, also of Esso Europe, who relinquished many a lunch hour to photostat the illustrations which we used in our workbooks; John Matthews of Phillips, Son and Neale for his cheerful willingness to search through old catalogues and files to extract photographs and descriptions of pieces sold in their premises as long as two decades ago; and the many people at Middlesex Polytechnic who by their happy tolerance and active help have made the long gestation period possible, with an extra tip of our hats to Doug Exell for his process photography, Pam Eldridge for her typing skills, and Peter Green for his continuing interest and encouragement.

But, above all, it is Henry Sandon to whom the greatest measure of appreciation must be given. It was he who insisted that this book had to be written and who, when the demands of our busy lives tempted us to put it all aside, gave us that necessary prod to get us back to it once again. And it is to Henry Sandon that we gratefully dedicate the product of our work.

L. O .B.
N. F.
J. S.

INTRODUCTORY

Chapter 1

A Brief View of Worcester Blue and White Wares

The Early Years

Valentine Green, writing in 1795[1]*, tells us that in the early days of the factory by far the bulk of production was decorated in blue. On the sole evidence of the quantities of blue and white ware surviving today, it seems beyond dispute that from the early 1750s through the following twenty-five years or so, the production of underglaze blue porcelain at Warmstry House must have reached staggering proportions.

It would seem that the principal form of decoration at Worcester's predecessors, Lund's factory in Bristol and its forerunner in Limehouse, was also in the cobalt blue. In March 1747, the *Daily Advertiser* of that City proclaimed:

To the Publick; The new-invented blue and white Limehouse ware . . . which as to duration, etc. is in no way inferior to China . . . at their manufactory, near Dick shore in Limehouse.[2]

Dr Richard Pococke, celebrated traveller of that era, wrote to his mother in November 1750 to give her an account of these Bristol wares. He refers to two sorts of china being made there, one being 'Whiter and I suppose this is made of a Calcin'd Flint and the Soapy rock at Lizard Point which 'tis known they use. This is painted blue.'[3] However, his main interest appeared to be in the 'fine ornamental china' from that factory, and no mention is made of coloured wares.

*See p. 28 for References to Chapter 1.

Although it can be very difficult to distinguish these early Bristol porcelains from those made at Worcester shortly thereafter, there are several differing characteristics which can assist identification. The Lund's Bristol blue tends to be darker in tone than that of Worcester, with a hint of indigo; and the glaze is much thicker, resulting in a hazy appearance, with a consequent blurring in the design. Sometimes this blurring can be so pronounced that the underlying pattern is indistinguishable. The Bristol paste is also more glassy than that developed later at Worcester, with a harder, greyer look when exposed. Archaeological evidence from the earliest levels of excavation at Worcester has shown that the Bristol paste was used by Worcester for at least a short while. Tests on wasters of this early paste indicate that the glost or glazing firing was done at a higher temperature than the initial biscuit firing, and this would explain the greater tendency to blur than would have occurred had the decoration been 'hardened-on', as later happened.[4]

Chinese landscapes make up nearly all of the known designs on these Bristol wares, and, although they are closely related, it is almost impossible to link any of these together so as to characterise them as patterns. There is, however, one attribute which occurs on a number of definite Bristol pieces; this is a motif of three dots arranged in a triangle, usually prominent in the design and often appearing more than once in the same panel. These designs, possibly derived from Chinese originals, are attributed to an unknown 'Three-

Dot Painter', and are as near as the Bristol factory came to producing a pattern. Other features distinguishing this painter are a group of mountains drawn in an unmistakable manner and the usual presence of fine large boats with dark sails. It is quite conceivable that certain arrangements on one piece could have been repeated on other examples, but generally the blue painting at Bristol is imaginative and varied.

The bankruptcy of Benjamin Lund led to the transfer of his machinery and effects from Bristol to Worcester in February 1752. The 'Worcester Tonquin Manufacture', as it was originally called, had been formed by deed of partnership in June 1751. Therefore, we find a gap of six to eight months during which it is not known whether or not there was any production of china at the Worcester works or, if so, what it was. One possible clue, now unfortunately lost, was a tureen which was noted and illustrated by R. W. Binns in 1878.[5] This tureen, he says, was white and undecorated except for the date '1751' painted in blue under its base. In shape, it matches a decorated tureen in the Dyson Perrins Collection in Worcester (see Pattern 1.A.11), but neither of these were found to correspond to a mould for a similar soup tureen still preserved at the Worcester Works Museum.

Interestingly, about the time Binns's book was published, there was some difference of view as to whether these finished tureens had been made at Worcester or whether they were of Bow manufacture. This dispute was resolved only when that great collector, Dyson Perrins, dared to break a piece from his own example and subject it to test, proving beyond doubt that it was of a soapstone, and therefore a Worcester body. The question still remains, of course, as to whether Binns's dated tureen was Worcester or Bristol. Based on the equivalence of the moulding on the tureen as illustrated by Binns to that of the certain Worcester example owned by Perrins, our own view is that this dated tureen was more likely to have been made at the Worcester factory. If this is so, it indicates that even in its initial months of operation, the Worcester craftsmen were capable of producing fine blue and white wares. Assuming

of course that the date '1751' was the actual date of manufacture, it is the earliest example of Worcester blue and white, and one can only regret that this unique piece of documentary history is now lost to us.

The earliest pieces of Worcester blue and white, dated by style and shape to the early 1750s, are naïve and crude by any comparison with the examples of the later years of that decade. These tend to be Chinese in influence, and usually depict Oriental figures or birds set in landscape backgrounds. It is tempting to see in these early wares the hand of a Bristol Delft painter, and indeed this may have been the case. When the Bristol factory was purchased in 1752 and brought to Worcester, a number of its workmen would almost certainly have moved there also. Even Benjamin Lund, the former proprietor, is recorded as being in Worcester in 1753 when his occupation was described as 'China maker'. Worcester designs such as 'The Lady with a Stormcloud' (Pattern I.A.2), 'The Writhing Rock' (Pattern I.A.5), 'The Squirrel and Vine' (Pattern I.C.32), and 'The Crescent Moon' (Pattern I.B.4), among others, show many of the characteristics found in the Bristol Delft painting. 'The Squirrel and Vine' is a design closely associated with the Bristol school; two of the other three patterns mentioned follow Bristol in the use of flocks of birds to fill in blank spaces, often seen on the Delft but not nearly so frequently on porcelain.

A clear example of Delft-style painting on Worcester is the well-known bowl formerly in the collection of Francis and Cecele Burrell and illustrated here as Pattern I.B.29. The painting depicts a figure in European dress standing on a jetty of stone blocks, with the characteristic birds in a cloudy sky and an elaborately naturalistic tree, all motifs strongly linked to Delft treatment. The painting is so different from any style found on other Worcester examples that one must conclude that the artist acquired his training elsewhere. Similar painting is found on some rare Reid's Liverpool porcelains, another centre for English Delft manufacture.

The early style of Worcester underglaze blue painting can often be close to that of Bristol, with simple, highly stylized landscapes and Oriental figures. 'The Willow Root' design (Pattern I.A.3) is typical of this, with twin mountains in the distance and a solid shaded foreground. The figure in this pattern (when it occurs at all) lacks the detail found on the later Worcester painted chinoiseries. Like Bristol, the design includes a predictable range of subjects, the fence, figure, willow tree, leaves and boats, but often arranged quite differently from example to example with parts omitted. This treatment, too, is reminiscent of Bristol painting, particularly that attributed to the 'Three-Dot Painter'. The large punch pot decorated with 'The Man with a Lunchbox' pattern, which is illustrated as Pattern I.A.24, also reflects this subject range, combining elements from three separate designs, 'The Crescent Moon' (Pattern I.B.4), 'The Willow Root', and 'The Man with a Parasol' (Pattern I.A.25). Further, the earliest levels reached in the Worcester factory site excavations produced a biscuit waster from a dish made of Bristol-type paste which was painted in unfired cobalt and illustrated a ship strongly resembling those found in the work of the 'Three-Dot Painter', so it is conceivable, even probable, that this same artist moved to Worcester following the closure at Lund's, and continued painting there in the same style as before.

Apart from a few of these 'Willow Root' type patterns that appear to have been made at the commencement of the Worcester factory in 1751–3, the Worcester blue is far better controlled than that of Bristol and its colour is a less harsh, pale, almost greyish blue. It is not possible to tell whether or not this colour difference is due to the absence of a 'hardening-on' firing of the Bristol wares or for some other reason. The wasters from the earliest Worcester excavation levels show that, after painting, the biscuit china was fired again, probably in the cooler lower areas of the glost kiln, and that this resulted in a fusing of the cobalt into the biscuit body. Without this 'hardening-on' firing, the cobalt colouration was likely to flow, both blurring the pattern on the piece itself and affecting other pieces in the kiln at the same time. Available evidence suggests that Bristol did not use this extra firing, and indeed could not do so in a process where the glaze was fired at a higher temperature than was the biscuit.

While blue was the only colour which could be used successfully as an underglaze decoration, Worcester nevertheless experimented with the use of other colours. Manganese was one of these, and the aubergine colour which it produced is known on Bristol and Bristol-type wares painted with sketchy landscapes as well as on a few rare examples of 'The Dragon' design (Pattern I.C.31). The 1977 excavation at Worcester produced two fragments decorated with an obviously experimental underglaze green, but the colour produced was very pale, and it is unlikely that any examples were actually produced for sale.

The Middle Period

With access to the comprehensive blue and white collections of the Dyson Perrins and Victoria and Albert Museums, as well as to a few of the specialist private collections, it has been possible to group together pieces of Worcester made in different periods and select from these items of a similar colour and type. This comparison indicates that there was a gradual change, probably beginning around 1755, towards a more simplified or stylized pattern, using a blue colouration which was a bit darker and more clearly defined, leading eventually to a point in about 1760 where the patterns became both heavier and darker—with larger and flatter areas of colour. This can be seen by looking through the patterns illustrated hereafter according to their probable date of manufacture. Some of the changes that become noticeable in this Middle Period can perhaps best be demonstrated in our illustrations of 'The Prunus Root' (Pattern I. D.27) where we have shown two pictures of bowls decorated with this design, the conical shaped piece being a paler blue with much more freedom to its painting. You will see that the 'root' itself becomes more rounded in the later example, whereas in the earlier conical bowl it has more twists and curls. The earlier flower sprays, too, are charmingly irregular, while those on the later 1770s bowl have reverted to a much more stylized and patterned form. Other patterns, too, such as 'The Landslip' (Pattern I.D.21) show a similar gradual transition whereby the earlier irregularities in the formation of the tree branches and buildings are removed in favour of a greater design uniformity.

The result of the formalization was surely a loss of the charming quality of the earlier wares, but nevertheless must have helped the increase of the factory's production, which, after all, was the purpose of the enterprise. By the quantities produced, there was clearly a great demand in the market-place for blue and white wares, unfortunately accompanied by a shortage of available skilled artists, the better painters already being required for the polychrome decoration. Consequently, by making a pattern simpler and quicker to paint, the factory management would have been able to produce the needed extra quantities of output with the use of the less capable artists. By 1765 or thereabouts, some of the Worcester designs had become so very simplified that they could virtually be mass-produced. 'The Cannonball', for example (Pattern I.D.6), was made up of a number of plain light and dark areas with only child-like buildings, and was consequently one of the least exacting patterns to paint. A certain Mrs Lybbe Powys who visited the factory in the 1760s, wrote of the large number of children who were employed in the works,[6] and it was undoubtedly some of these who were responsible for the rapid painting of the blue designs. Even so, by 1761 there must have been a shortage of good china painters available at Worcester, for on both 12 and 15 December 1761, editions of *The London General Evening Post* carried the following advertisement:

Wanted: Painters in Blue and White: Good Workmen, who are sober and diligent, will meet with proper encouragement, by applying to the manufactory in Worcester.[7]

The great demand for blue and white ware was undoubtedly linked to the fact that it sold for a relatively reasonable price. The first reference to the sale of Worcester porcelain appeared in an advertisement in *The Bath Advertiser* on January 31 1756:

Bristol, January 24. This is to give notice that I have lately purchased a large assortment of enamel'd and Blue and White useful Worcester China ware which will be sold, at the Warehouse in Castle Green, cheaper, better in quality and in greater variety than has hitherto been exposed to sale there.[8] The lowest price will be marked on each piece of ware, according as it is more or less perfect, without Abatement, unless to wholesale dealers, who shall be allowed a discount for present money . . . which will make it greatly their interest to deal for this ware, with their humble servant Robert Carpenter, N.B. Good Blue and White Tea Cups and Saucers, at 3s 6d per set, Quart Basons 10d, Half Pints 7d, and all other sorts in proportion.[9]

The fame of Worcester's good quality blue and white soon spread. In February 1758, Benjamin Franklin wrote to his wife, Deborah, from England to tell her of some English porcelain that he was sending to her:

Melons and leaves for a desert of fruit and cream, or the like; a bowl remarkable for the neatness of the figures made at Bow near this City, some coffee cups of the same; a Worcester bowl, ordinary.

He goes on to mention:

A large fine jug for beer, to stand in the cooler. I fell in love with it at first sight; for I thought it looked like a fat jolly dame, clean and tidy, with a neat blue and white calico gown on, good natured and lovely, and put me in mind of somebody.[10]

Look now at the large jug which we illustrate with 'The Cabbage-Leaf Jug Floral' (Pattern I.E.21), and surely the same image will come to your mind, as it did to Ben Franklin's.

In May 1763, the *Oxford Journal* wrote of Worcester porcelain and its qualities:

. . . services of Chinese porcelain may be made up with Worcester so that the difference can not be discovered. The great abuse of it is the selling of other far inferior kinds of ware for Worcester, by which both the buyer is deceived to his loss and the credit of the manufacture is injured. The most valuable part of all, and which principally calls for notice, is the extraordinary strength and cheapness of the common sort of blue and white Worcester porcelain; and let any person but impartially consider the difference, in these respects, between this and that of an equil degree, though hardly of equil beauty, imported from abroad, and he will find the advantage is considerable and in favour of the former, that if he has any degree of candour, he must see and acknowledge his obligations to a manufacture which not only supplies an ornament fitted for the homes and cabinets of the rich and curious, but affords an elegant and desirable furniture calculated by its ease of purchase, for general and ordinary use.[11]

It is difficult to determine with any precision just how expensive Worcester blue and white ware really was, as no factory order-books survive. However, in June 1772, a shop in Bath placed the following advertisement:

Now on Sale . . . at Mainwarings, complete Tea Services of Blue and White Worcester China, from £1.15s. the set, consisting of 43 pieces.[12]

This same shop also sold Chinese porcelains, and in 1778 a set of forty-three pieces of Chinese blue and white teawares cost £1. 9s., so it can be seen that the Worcester service was fairly competitive with the cheap imported Chinese wares whose prices, almost unbelievably, remained attractive despite the imposition of import duties, transportation and warehousing costs and substantial auctioneer and dealer commissions. These 43-piece sets, whether Oriental or English, would normally comprise a teapot with cover and a teapot stand (in the later services), sucrier (sugar bowl) with cover, slop bowl, jug, spoon tray, two cakeplates, twelve teacups or teabowls, twelve coffee cups, and twelve saucers.

In 1769, the now famous Mr Christie sold in his London auction rooms on behalf of the factory 'A large and elegant assortment of the Worcester porcelain', the sale lasting for six days, according to the sale catalogue as quoted by Nightingale.[13] There was little blue and white ware in the sale, but among the items listed were 'Two Blue and White Sallad Dishes, two double handled Sauceboats and two Goss Lettuce ditto', all sold for 10s.

6d. 'Two Blue and White Cabbage leaves, four vine leaves, for compotiers and two candlesticks' fetched 12s. In the same sale, 'A service of fifteen oblong dishes, five sizes, blue sprig pattern' sold for £2. 4s., and a 'Dessert set ditto containing nine compotiers' realized £1. 2s. Almost certainly these were of 'The Pine Cone Group' (Pattern II.C.11), so often found on large dishes of this kind. The only actual reference to a particular pattern is a 'Blue and White Jar and Cover and two Beakers, Weeping Willow'. These were purchased for 6s. 6d. This was possibly 'The Landslip' design (Pattern I.D.21), or alternatively, in view of the date, 'The Candle Fence' decoration (Pattern I.D.18), both of which feature prominent willow trees, although we have no contemporary records of either being used on vases.

As can be seen, the prices obtained for the blue and white pieces are not excessive, and certainly were far below those quoted for the polychrome-decorated wares. Their ability to compete with the prices of the imported Chinese porcelains is surely evidence of the successful mass production methods used at the factory during this period, both through simplifying the painting requirements and, most importantly, by the development of transfer-printing.

It is not certain who first introduced the process of transfer-printing to Worcester, but the technique was first used, with onglaze wares, in the so-called black 'Smokey Primitives' that date from around 1753–5. Development of the printing technique was rapid, and by 1757, the date of the first onglaze 'King of Prussia' prints, the factory had achieved a remarkably high standard, both in the etching of the copper plates and in the transferring methods. These onglaze black prints remained very popular for a considerable period.

The underglaze blue transfer-prints, however, were slower in development and do not begin to appear until the late 1750s. W.M. Binns, writing in 1909, notes:

In the year 1770 it is a matter of history that there was a serious strike upon the Worcester works amongst the artists who had been employed in executing the blue and white decorations by hand, against the printing press, by which they were deprived of their work, and in consequence many of them left the manufactory. It is hardly likely that the painters waited some years before they forcibly demonstrated their objections to the printing press.[14]

Binns concludes, therefore, that the blue printing only came into great use around 1770, and probably was employed only occasionally before that time. Certainly, we know that underglaze blue was being used at the factory much before that time, but his story of the artists' strike (which he took from his father, R.W. Binns)[15] may well have been accurate. In February 1770, for example, *Berrow's Worcester Journal* carried this advertisement:

CHINA WARE PAINTERS WANTED for the Plymouth New Invented Patent Porcelain Manufactory. A number of sober ingenious artists, capable of painting in enamel and blue, may hear of constant employment by sending their proposals to Thomas Frank, in Castle Street, Bristol.[16]

It is quite possible that some of these Worcester artists did leave the factory and accept employment at Plymouth, for many of the Worcester-style designs were produced there, some so close in treatment to the original that one can conclude they were without doubt painted by former Worcester craftsmen. Others of these disgruntled artists probably made their way to the Derby factory where painting skills were also much in demand. Despite these depredations, however, blue and white painting continued in considerable quantity at Worcester for many years, albeit with a reduced quality.

The development of the blue printing technique from the 1750s onward was shown clearly by the products from the excavations of the Warmstry House site, and perhaps this would be the best occasion to mention the significance of the 'wasters', or broken fragments of porcelain, which were uncovered there. The intention of the several excavations that took place on the site of the original factory was to seek the earliest levels at which factory artifacts could be found and thus help to explode the popular myth that virtually all of the 'famille rose' type patterns of the early 1750s

had actually been made at Bristol, as had much of the early blue and white wares. In the 1969 excavation, some of the levels dating from the 1750 decade were reached, and the findings from these are fully described by Henry Sandon's work on early Worcester Porcelain, to which the reader is referred.[17]

By 1977, the level of the River Severn had receded beyond that experienced in 1969, and it was decided to mount another excavation on a different part of the factory site. Unfortunately, only levels of the later 1750s were reached here, but a series of stratified deposits dating from about 1755 to 1762 were located, and the finds from these and other slightly later levels can now be dated with some accuracy. The table opposite lists the blue and white patterns that were found at these various levels.

Obviously, this list does not represent a complete range of the patterns produced within these dates, but it does give us some important data. For example, we can see that 'The Man in the Pavilion' (Pattern II.B.1) was probably the first blue and white landscape print produced, dating from as early as 1757–8, but that it had a relatively short lifespan. Several pieces of the design were found in levels 18 and 17, but none were uncovered after 1760. So, the pattern can be given a date range from about 1757 to 1760. 'The Plantation Print' (Pattern II.B.5) takes its place around 1760, being the only printed design found in level 15, and was still in production in 1765, when it was joined by 'The Fence' (Pattern II.B.9), along with unidentified, large, naturalistic flower spray patterns. In the 1969 excavation, this print was recorded as occurring about 1770, and, in the 1977 excavation, was not found in level 8, about 1775. The probable date range which we can give to 'The Plantation Print' then, is from about 1760 to 1770, on the basis of the data above.

It is by this same method that many of the patterns listed in this book have been given a date range, although there will be exceptions to these because of historical gaps left unfilled by evidence from these excavations. For example, no levels after about 1780 could be accurately dated, and so the probable discontinuation date of certain

Level	Date	Printed Patterns	Painted Patterns
19	*c.* 1757	None	Various Floral Sprays
18	1757–58	Man in the Pavilion	Prunus Root Mansfield Cannonball Plantation
17	1758–60	Man in the Pavilion	Cannonball Prunus Root Mansfield
15	*c.* 1760	Plantation Print	Prunus Root Mansfield Cannonball Landslip Feather Mould Floral Bird in a Ring Reeded Shapes with Border
13	*c.* 1765	Plantation Print Fence Large Natural Florals	Cannonball Prunus Root Mansfield Feather Mould Floral Reeded Shapes with Border Hollow Rock Lily Bird in a Ring Pickle Leaf Vine Blind Earl Little Fisherman
8	*c.* 1775	Fence Three Flowers Fisherman and Cormorant Birds in Branches Mother and Child Fruit and Wreath Pine Cone Group Gilliflower Print Large Natural Florals Various Landscapes	Cannonball Mansfield Late Floral Sprigs Prunus Root Rock Strata Island Reeded Shapes with Border Precipice Peony Feather Mould Floral Hollow Rock Lily Candle Fence Two Quails Royal Lily Chantilly Sprig Doughnut Tree Pickle Leaf Vine Two Porter Landscape

common patterns, e.g. 'The Prunus Root' (Pattern I.D.27) and Cannonball' (Pattern I.D.6), have to be estimated from surviving examples.

Similar logic can be applied to roughly determine the rarity of patterns as well, although the waster pits uncovered during the excavations are not altogether representative of the actual production of that time. Nevertheless, by counting the number of wasters decorated with each pattern, a rank order can be obtained which does seem to reflect probable quantities of each produced, and thus the comparative rarity of the patterns involved:

Level 13, c. 1765

Pattern	No. of Wasters	Percentage
The Cannonball	280	30.2
Reeded Shapes with Border	139	15.0
Mansfield	120	12.9
The Prunus Root	90	9.7
Large Natural Floral Prints	84	9.1
The Plantation Print	59	6.4
The Fence	55	5.9
The Hollow Rock Lily	30	3.2
The Bird in a Ring	22	2.4
The Pickle Leaf Vine	17	1.8
The Two Porter Landscape	11	1.2
Others	20	2.2

Level 8, c. 1775

Pattern	No. of Wasters	Percentage
The Fence	156	20.4
The Three Flowers	113	14.8
The Cannonball	80	10.5
Mansfield	68	8.9
The Fisherman and Cormorant	39	5.1
Painted Floral Sprigs	26	3.4
The Prunus Root	22	2.9
Reeded Shapes with Border	21	2.8
The Birds in Branches	20	2.6
The Mother and Child	19	2.5
The Rock Strata Island	18	2.4
The Peony	18	2.4
Others	163	21.4

In 1765, you can see that the painted patterns like 'The Cannonball', 'Mansfield', and 'The Prunus Root' (Patterns I.D.6, I.E.1, and I.D.27, respectively), as well as the painted border patterns on the reeded shapes occur far more frequently than any of the printed patterns, while in 1775 the position has reversed with 'The Fence' (Pattern II.B.9) and 'The Three Flowers' (Pattern II.C.19) becoming by far the most common. By comparing the substantial quantities of the painted and printed patterns at the various levels, a picture of the development of transfer-printing can be seen:

	Percentage Printed	Percentage Painted
Level 19, c. 1757	—	100.0
Level 18, c. 1757–58	10.0	90.0
Level 17, c. 1758–60	13.2	86.8
Level 15, c. 1760	12.5	87.5
Level 13, c. 1765	28.0	72.0
Level 8, c. 1775	77.2	22.8

After a slow beginning, then, there is a marked increase in printed production between 1765 and 1775, resulting in printing becoming the principal form of decoration. So, perhaps Binns's account of the 1770 artists' strike is correct, as it appears from the rapid growth of transfer-printing at Worcester that they had cause for concern.

The first blue and white transfer-prints are somewhat simplistic and lack the sophistication of the onglaze print engravings associated with Robert Hancock. The first evidence of Hancock's hand in the underglaze blue prints is in the large flower spray designs introduced around 1760. These florals resemble the botanical illustrations done for use in the popular books of that time, and may well have been based on the plates which Hancock had etched for use in such volumes as *The Ladies' Amusement*, a frequent source for ceramic designs. These early prints are followed by the further vast range of floral sprays produced in the mid-1760s.

One of the drawbacks of printed patterns is that a different copper plate had to be prepared for every shape of porcelain upon which the pattern was to be used. The standard tea service of forty-three pieces would require then, ten engraved plates for the main design, plus additional engravings for covers and for the ornaments used on handles and spouts. Painted patterns, on the other hand, could be adapted by any talented artist to fit whatever shape was at hand. This problem was partially resolved by preparing prints of separate flower sprays to be placed on several different shapes and varied by the rearrangement of the subsidiary sprigs and borders. During the 1760s, these floral sprays assumed great popularity, with 'The Three Flowers' design of the 1770s eventually ranking as one of the most prolifically used of all the Worcester patterns, along with 'The Fence' and 'The Pine Cone Group' designs (Patterns II.B.9 and II.C.11). By reducing the number of plates required, the ever important costs of production could be further reduced, probably adding to the popularity of 'The Three Flowers' design, one of the least expensive printed patterns available.

There is a regrettable tendency to dismiss transfer-printed patterns as being somehow inferior to the painted designs, in our minds an unjustified prejudice. It is said that prints are, by their nature, unoriginal, and comparable only to any other mass-produced ware. Yet, when one takes into account the time, effort and skill required to finish an etched or engraved copper plate as compared with an equally complex and demanding painted design, it is quite evident that the printed piece has demanded the greater effort of accomplishment. Modern engravers at the Royal Worcester Works estimate, for example, that a copper plate for 'The Fence' pattern would require between twenty and twenty-four hours to engrave, while a saucer of the similar but painted 'Cannonball' design would take an experienced painter no more than thirty minutes to execute. On the other hand, the copper plate would have a lifespan of 600–800 'pulls', and therefore, the painted piece would have taken fifteen times as long as the time spent on each printed saucer.

One thing that is immediately apparent when examining the wide range of painted designs used at Worcester is the almost incredible care with which the standard of each pattern is reproduced. Although the treatment of a design can vary from one painter to another, the pattern arrangement rarely varies to any noticeable degree. The factory management was clearly concerned that a complete service should be matched in every way, and that replacement or supplementary pieces could be ordered with satisfaction in this regard. This standard, however, was accomplished only through the sacrifice of the spontaneity and artistic freedom which, for instance, can be seen on some of the 'one off' landscapes produced by competitors in Liverpool.

Worcester, of course, was quite prepared to produce these 'one off' designs on special order. Usually, the shapes used for these individual pieces were mugs, and their inscriptions and dates are of great importance in our study of the blue and white wares. The earliest known dated piece (with the exception of the very early dated tureen described by Binns above) is a coffee can or small mug in the British Museum collection which is painted with 'The Union Jack House' design (Pattern I.B.1) and inscribed beneath 'T. B. 1753'. Since the pattern was used on other uninscribed pieces as well, it appears that the factory here has only added the inscription as a special order. The next dated service, of which several pieces survive, is also of a standard pattern. This is a miniature or 'toy' tea service decorated with 'The Prunus Root' pattern, and inscribed below 'C. S. 1757'. It is reputed to have been made for the young Charlotte Sherriff at about that date. Following these early pieces are a number of examples which are definitely in the 'one off' category, and made to specific instructions of the client. A 'scratch-cross' (i.e. spreading base) type of small mug or coffee can in the Dyson Perrins Museum collection is inscribed:

> I drink up the liquor
> Tho the cup is but small
> And heres a good health
> To Edmund Wall

undoubtedly a presentation piece for a member of Dr John Wall's own family. Another mug, also at the Dyson Perrins Museum, is painted with an elaborate cartouche and angel head, with the name 'Peter Taylor 1769'. The British Museum owns a mug painted with the Arms of the Freemasons, the only underglaze blue specimen known among a wide range of identified coloured armorials.

However, most of the inscribed pieces tend to follow a definite type which were made to order in the 1770s. By that time, the factory had developed a very formal floral painting style exemplified by 'The Gilliflower/The Narcissus' (Pattern I.E.12). As a general rule, the Gilliflower and the Narcissus motifs were interchangeable, and sometimes were replaced altogether by a cypher and date – for example, the mug at the Dyson Perrins which is inscribed:

$$S + B$$
$$1776$$

Several of this type of inscribed mugs are known, using only the subsidiary sprigs from 'The Gilliflower/The Narcissus' design. In one of these, the scattered sprigs surround the motif of a lamb and a flag, the crest of Sir John Davie. Another type of inscribed piece of which four examples are known are the 'St George and the Dragon' mugs (Pattern I.A.34). Three of these are inscribed around the foot or under the base 'Ann. Dunn Bir^{m}' and are dated either 1775 or 1776. The other has no inscription other than the date, 1776. Again, they are decorated with the same subsidiary sprigs.

The final type of inscribed pieces are those which have been transfer-printed with a standard pattern and are then painted with the inscription required. Typical examples are two mugs, one in the Godden Reference Collection and the other owned by the authors, each of which has the printed 'La Pêche/La Promenade Chinoise' design (Pattern II.A.10) with 'Iohn Izod Stratford 1780' written under the handle. It should be mentioned however, that whereas the Lowestoft factory specialized in inscribed and dated pieces, all Worcester examples are exceedingly rare, since that factory looked to a market further afield filled with customers happy with the ownership of standard patterns at reasonable prices.

The Davis-Flight Period

During the latter half of the 1770s, there seems to have been some change in the material used at Worcester for underglaze blue decoration, for a considerable change in colour had now occurred. The dark inky-blue of the 1760s had given way to a much brighter colour with a slight violet or indigo tinge, and an apparently greater tendency to run or blur. The reason for the change is not known, and was probably due to the use of a different smalt mixture, the cobalt oxide used to achieve the blue colouration. Dr John Wall had died in 1776, having retired the year previously, and the factory was now in the control of William Davis, one of the original partners. Davis was an astute businessman and was unlikely to agree to any change of materials unless convinced that it would benefit the profitability of the enterprise. The quantities of these 'Davis-Flight' examples that exist today tell us that they must have been abundantly produced, although many collectors have ignored them because of the lesser quality they represent and the unpleasing and over harsh colour with which they are decorated. In 1775, both Thomas Turner and Robert Hancock, two of the stalwarts of the Worcester business, had left to form their own establishment at Caughley in Shropshire, and by 1775 were producing blue and white wares there in sharp competition with Worcester. This may have led Davis to try to reduce his costs by using a less expensive cobalt material, although it is equally persuasive to maintain that the new colour was simply more fashionable, and thereby more saleable.

Even the most ardent Worcester admirer is forced to admit that the quality of the transfer-printing done during this period was, as often as not, abysmal. Joseph Lygo, a china salesman, wrote to William Duesbury at the Derby factory: 'Mr. Turner . . . manufactures more fine goods than Flights', and, referring to his requirement for a stock of chamber pots, '. . . I have not had an opportunity of going into the city to enquire at the Worcester warehouse if they have them, but if they have they will be much worse than the Staffordshire ones.'[18]

The Davis-Flight period also brought about a change in the type of patterns used. Although the popular prints of 'The Fence', 'The Three Flowers' and 'The Fruit Sprigs' (Pattern II.C.25) remained in demand, new types of a heavy Chinese design were being introduced, possibly influenced by Caughley's success with their use. 'The Mother and Child' (Pattern II.A.13) and 'The Fisherman and Cormorant' (Pattern II.A.19) were among the first of these new style designs dating from around 1775, and these were to be joined and eventually replaced by such further patterns as 'The Argument' (Pattern II.B.10), 'The Bandstand' (Pattern II.B.12), and 'The Bat' (Pattern II.B.26). These latter designs are distinguished by their very elaborate borders and characteristic hand washing-in of the foreground colour in replacement of the normal finely hatched lines, a method used also at Lowestoft but not at Caughley. These heavy Worcester patterns usually have a disguised numeral mark and date from around 1780.

During this period the use of painted patterns decreased steadily and, apart from a few formal designs such as 'The Royal Lily' (Pattern I.F.8) and 'The Music' (Pattern I.F.11), were restricted to the floral sprig decorations like 'The Gilliflower/The Narcissus'. This late formal style of floral sprig was frequently used as a space filler with a number of patterns after the late 1770s, and could be used to decorate pieces not otherwise suitable for painting, such as the stem and foot areas of eyebaths or between the panels of patterns like 'The Strap Flute Sauceboat Floral' (Pattern I.E.37).

Just as contemporary tastes changed in favour of the brighter Davis-Flight blue, the polychrome decoration began to outsell the blue and white wares. In order to sell many of the printed patterns, it became necessary to embellish them with gilding to give them a richer appearance. Sometimes this could be accomplished simply by the addition of a gold line around the border, but 'The Bat' and a few other patterns occasionally can be found with the principal design fully picked out in gold. Some of the gilding was added by the Chamberlain establishment at Worcester, which prior to the making of their own porcelains,

bought wares from other factories in England for further decoration; their primary source for these was the Caughley factory, but goods were also purchased from Flights as well. Many of Chamberlain's early records still survive, and some of these refer to the Worcester blue and white wares.[19] For example, in November 1788 Chamberlain placed an order for:

2 sets of landskip blue edg	5/4
2 sets of Ruins	5/4
2 sets of Milk Maid, gold edg	12/-

all involving patterns unique to Worcester and not made at Caughley. Other entries in the 1788–90 records refer to patterns named 'Worc[r] Temple', 'Landscape circled', or 'circled landscape', 'Parrott', 'Worcester Pomgran[ate] or Fruit', 'Fruit and Wreath', 'Birds (blue edg)', and 'Royal Lily', all of which can be identified with known Worcester patterns of this period. The pattern which we now know as 'The Fisherman and Cormorant' was referred to by Chamberlain as 'Pleasure Boat' or variously 'P Boat', a pattern also made in great quantities by the Caughley factory. In November 1788, Chamberlain wrote to Thomas Turner at Caughley asking for 'no more 2nd size Teas P. Boat unless they can be sent at the Worc[r] price 5/6' and, again 'Pleasure Boat seconds 2nd size charged 4*s* per set, only 3/8 Worcester prize' (*sic*). So it seems that Worcester was able to price competitively, even against the mass production methods of its Caughley rival.

Nevertheless, in order to sell these wares it was necessary for Chamberlain to add gold, and most of his stock at the time was of these heavily printed chinoiserie designs. The simple blue and white patterns of twenty years before had become unsaleable altogether. To combat this problem and dispose of the inventories of the earlier wares, several decorators seized upon the idea of over-decorating their designs with onglaze colours, often paying little regard to the underlying pattern. This redecoration of the blue and white porcelain with colours, known as 'clobbering', may well have been carried out at the Worcester factory itself, as well as in other English establishments, who also were adding colours to their stocks of Chinese porcelains at the same time.

Although the decline in the demand for the blue and white wares certainly was a discouragement to their further production, this is only part of the story. John Flight, who had purchased the factory from Davis in 1783, wrote in his diary for July 19 1789:

Have had a good deal of trouble the last week about the Blue printing, the colours peel off in the burning-in and spoils a vast deal of ware. Every possible attention is payed to it to find out the cause and remidy it, but hitherto without success.[20]

The increasing competition in the form of cheap, blue-printed, Staffordshire earthenware probably was the final blow that sealed the fate of Worcester's blue wares. By the mid-1790s, under-glaze blue as a form of decoration was virtually finished at Worcester, being retained only to add dark flowerheads, butterflies and borders to what were basically gold designs, all of these painted in a highly stylized manner. These blue and gold patterns usually bear the incised 'B' or a very small open crescent mark, and were not produced in any numbers after the eighteenth century.

A Note on Marks

One of the most fascinating aspects of Worcester's blue and white wares are the marks that appear upon them. A very large percentage of the pieces were marked in some way, and the meaning of these marks remains one of the most confused and puzzling areas in all of English ceramic study.

During the 1750s, many of the Worcester pieces will be found to have workmen's marks which take a wide variety of forms. Indeed, the variety appears unending, adding to the difficulty of trying to understand their significance. It would be comforting to accept the long held belief that they are simply painter's marks, applied by the artist who decorated the piece, but we know that the answer is not that simple. Certain marks appear to fall within certain distinct groups, the primary ones being a number of versions of a 'TF' monogram, along with similar 'IH' or 'JH' monograms. Others which are frequently en-

countered are an arrow and annulet, often in combination, a mark resembling a musical note symbol, and various types of pseudo-Chinese symbols. There seems to be little doubt that some pieces which bear identical marks were painted by different hands, eliminating the notion that these were tied to an individual artist. Further, a number of pieces exist which have more than one mark; one cornucopia, for example, has been noted as having five different workmen's marks, yet was surely painted by a single hand.

There is a further theory that the marks in some way relate to the patterns which they accompany, and while there is a limited support for this view, it fails as a complete answer. It is true that certain patterns tend to be found with a particular worker's mark more frequently than with another; for instance, 'The Willow Root' (Pattern I.A.3) is most often marked with a psuedo-Chinese symbol, but it can also be found with others. Also, the variety of marks found with other patterns can be staggering. Therefore, until a great deal more study has been done here, it is really not possible to do more than speculate on their meaning. Are they related in some way to 'batches' of production, to the customers for whom they were destined, to departments of the factory, or are they 'tally' marks of some kind? At present, this must remain a mystery.

By around 1758 or possibly 1760, the workmen's marks had given way to the open painted crescent. We have seen no examples which can be dated after 1760 which bear workmen's marks, although one can find a badly drawn crescent which may have that appearance. It is difficult to be sure as to the probable date when the crescent mark was first introduced. The earliest use seems to be about 1757–8 when it can be found on primitive transfer-printed ware. Henry Sandon illustrates the arms of the Warmstry family whose house was later occupied by the factory and questions whether the crescents contained there might have been the inspiration for its use by the Worcester factory, but of course there is no way of being certain.[21] Surely by the mid-1760s the crescent was widely used as a mark on almost every piece of blue and white made. On the painted wares it is always drawn open, while on the printed pieces it will usually be found to be hatched. Like the anchor marks of the Chelsea factory, the Worcester crescent, both printed and painted, can vary greatly in size and shape.

Sometimes the printed crescent will be found to have an additional letter placed between the arms of the mark, these ranging from A through to G, with P and R also not uncommon, and more rarely, other letters as well. Certain numerals have also been used in place of the letters. You may find these additions on printed teawares made from around the mid-1770s, and, again, their significance is unknown. In one case, the printed crescent has been converted into a 'Man in the Moon' face; although sometimes illustrated as open, the crescent here is hatched, and derives from a copper plate engraved with 'The Fence' pattern and made around 1770 for prints to decorate saucers. At least six examples of these 'Man in the Moon' crescents are known, two of which are on factory wasters, and there is little doubt that they all originate from this one copper plate.

The purpose of the crescent mark becomes even more unclear when considering two biscuit wasters found in the excavations of the factory site. Both of these are bases of sucriers which were printed with 'The Fence' pattern, and on each there appears a crescent mark with an additional cerif at the top which transforms this into the letter 'C'. Caughley regularly used a 'C' mark but this Worcester 'C' is quite different from that, as well as slightly pre-dating the beginning of the Caughley works, so is unlikely to be an attempt to copy the Shropshire factory. No finished examples bearing this 'C' mark are known.

The 'W' mark, which was introduced in the 1760s and used until the late 1770s, presents less of a mystery. It is very occasionally found in a painted version, but was much more frequently printed, later taking on an elaborate script-scroll shape. Surprisingly, it was very little used in comparison with the crescent mark.

In about 1775–8, the first use of the disguised numeral marks is found on 'The Fisherman and Cormorant' pattern, and by the 1780s their use had become widespread. These are single digit numerals disguised by the addition of further lines so as to resemble Chinese characters, and are applied to a new style of blue and white printed patterns in the brighter coloured blue. The elaborate Chinese landscapes are perhaps aimed at a new market which had been established by the Caughley factory, and it has been suggested that these disguised numerals were brought into use so that regular clients would not know that these uncharacteristic wares were actually made at Worcester. Like the workmen's marks of thirty years earlier, the disguised numerals seem to have no relationship to either the pattern or its style. They range from 1 to 9.

All of the marks discussed so far, the crescents, the disguised numerals, the script and printed 'W', must surely rank as some kind of factory mark, as opposed to the mark of some individual craftsman. However, in addition to these, some patterns have their own unique mark which, in a way, must be regarded as an integral part of the overall design. Usually Chinese in style, these pattern marks were first used in the mid-1750s on such patterns as 'The Children at Play' (Pattern I.A.19). These designs are often direct copies of Chinese originals, as are the marks they employ. Others, such as the marks on 'The Fan-Panelled Landscape' (Pattern I.B.27), or 'The Hundred Antiques' (Pattern I.F.2) are clearly European in origin and have no relationship to the Oriental porcelains. Even these unique pattern marks have been the object of considerable speculation, with some authors suggesting that they were a form of factory date code, an idea which, while appealing, is completely without foundation.

So we are left with the conclusion that at present all we can do is to note the existence and the differences of these marks over the period, without any real understanding of their significance, leaving them for future study and interpretation.

Worcester's Contemporaries and Imitators

With the enormous popularity of blue and white porcelains at this time, it was inevitable that much competition would begin to emerge in the industry. Some of the manufacturers of this ware pre-dated the Worcester enterprise, and many others were quick to copy the already established styles. Although no useful purpose would be served to repeat details of the various eighteenth-century English porcelain manufacturers, most of which is already well known, it must be remembered that Worcester itself was a master copier of competitive designs, adapting many from the Chinese and certain of the Continental factories, as well as freely borrowing from the patterns which had originated in the English factories of Bow and Caughley. It is probably from Bow that Worcester's powder blue ground derives, and possibly its 'Dragon' pattern (Pattern I.C.31) as well, while Caughley's 'Bandstand', 'Temple' and certain floral sprig patterns each served as standards for the Worcester versions. Happily, however, most of the 'borrowing' was the other way around.

The painted patterns seemed to have been less frequently copied than were the printed ones, although such patterns as 'The Prunus Root' was made by Bow, Chaffer's Liverpool, Derby and Longton Hall, while 'Mansfield' was used by Bow, Caughley, Derby, Lowestoft and Plymouth. Derby 'adapted' several other Worcester patterns as well, notably the printed 'Fence' design and 'The Plantation Print', while Pennington's factory in Liverpool made several rather poor imitations of the Worcester patterns. But it was Caughley and Lowestoft who were Worcester's imitators.

Lowestoft copied most of Worcester's standard shapes and designs with such complete authenticity that many of the most experienced collectors can sometimes be misled. Copies were made of 'The Fence' 'The Three Flowers', 'The Pine Cone Group', 'The Natural Sprays Group' (Pattern II.C.7) 'Mansfield', 'Immortelle' (Pattern I.F.10), and even the ubiquitous 'Two Porter Landscape' (Pattern I.B.31), all using exact Worcester shapes. Many of these patterns will be found with a crescent mark, although this is always open and never hatched. The quality of the Lowestoft copies is almost always inferior to the Worcester originals, using a deep inky-blue and oppressively heavy printing, so in most instances should not present a problem for anyone who has handled several examples from each of the factories' wares. The same, however, is not true of the Caughley porcelain.

Thomas Turner, founder of the Caughley works, was trained at Worcester under the tutelage of Robert Hancock, who followed his former pupil to the Shropshire factory in 1775. It is not surprising, therefore, to find the paste used at Caughley to be quite similar to that of Worcester, both being of a steatite body. Although the Caughley blue tends to be darker and more inky, the quality of the painting done at that factory can be equally fine. Most of the Worcester transfer-prints were used at Caughley as well, and were often so closely copied that the design alone gives no clues in distinguishing the two. The early production of the Caughley establishment can be so similar to that of Worcester that examples of patterns such as 'The Rock Strata Island' (Pattern I.D.8) and 'The Waiting Chinaman' (Pattern I.A.6) have frequently passed through the London salerooms described as Worcester, and large baskets or junket dishes decorated with 'The Pine Cone' design are such close reproductions of the Worcester original that even the most experienced collectors must take a second look. Caughley freely used Worcester's 'chrysanthemum' moulding, printing rather than painting the central flower and border; they also produced printed versions of Worcester's painted patterns 'Mansfield' and 'Peony' (Pattern I.E.7), as well as of Worcester's vine-leaf pickle tray designs. Robert Hancock's talents can be seen in many of the Caughley transfer-prints such as 'La Pêche/La Promenade Chinoise', although it is unlikely that these were done from the same plates used at Worcester during Hancock's employment there. 'The Fisherman and Cormorant' pattern was used by both makers, with only minor differences. For a detailed description of the Caughley patterns and their comparisons with those of Worcester, you should certainly read Geoffrey Godden's very comprehensive work on this subject.[22]

When Caughley marked their wares, they used either a printed 'C' or a letter 'S', but occasionally you will find a painted 'C'. This latter mark can resemble the Worcester open crescent, but invariably has a distinct bar at its top, a feature sometimes found on badly drawn Worcester marks and leading to some possible hindrance in identification. No pieces of Caughley are known which use a printed hatched crescent.

Therefore, when attempting to identify a piece of blue and white, one should first examine its base. If it has a printed crescent or a 'W' mark, you may safely conclude that it is of Worcester origin. If it is marked with an open crescent or has no mark at all, you should then turn your attention to its footrim. A Worcester footrim will be triangular in form, whereas the Caughley rim will appear as long and square. On Worcester and Caughley examples, the glaze on the base will be shiny, and will have been 'pegged' or wiped away, leaving a glaze free margin, unlike examples made at Lowestoft. Further, the Lowestoft footrims are susceptible to staining, and their bases rarely show any trace of an incised centre ring, caused by turning, frequently found on the Worcester and Caughley thrown and turned shapes.

With the exception of Pennington's, few of the Liverpool factories copied Worcester directly, although there can be some confusion in distinguishing the products of the Chaffer's and Christian's factories from those of Worcester. This is because their pastes were also of soapstone, often like that of Worcester and thus easily mistaken. Most of the blue colour used by these factories however is of a greyer tone than that of Worcester, and the paste and glaze tend to reflect a greenish tint. The Pennington porcelain can only be described as 'messy' and poorly fired, and its printing is of such inferior quality that it would be quite difficult to confuse it with almost any of the other factories. In addition, you should remember that the Liverpool porcelains are never marked in any way, while most of the Worcester wares will have a mark of some kind.

While we have deliberately avoided mentioning in the commentary accompanying the pattern photographs hereafter any of the imitations of the Worcester designs which appeared on earthenware (pottery) bodies, it should be noted that these can be found in fair quantities, both of eighteenth- and nineteenth-century manufacture. In the latter half of the 1700s, pearlware versions of such painted Worcester patterns as 'The Gilliflower' are quite common, and one will also find imitations of other painted designs such as 'The Cannonball' 'Mansfield', 'The Candle Fence' and 'The Rock Strata Island' (see index for pattern numbers). However, the most common designs imitated by the earthenware potteries of the eighteenth century were the printed patterns, the most frequently found being 'The Fence' and 'The Three Flowers'. Many of these will be marked with a copied printed crescent or 'C', but should never really be confused with the genuine porcelain originals. It is ironic of course that it was these eighteenth-century Staffordshire pearlwares which marked the eventual downfall in the popularity of the Worcester blue and white porcelains.

Mention should also be made of the reproductions of the eighteenth-century wares which were done in the following century by the Coalport factory and that of Booth in Stoke-on-Trent. R. W. Binns writes about these fakes in 1878:

Some of the blue and white ware of an Oriental pattern is stated to be made in Holland, but of this we have no evidence. Much of it has been unquestionably made in Staffordshire and Shropshire where the old marks, the crescent and the square, are regularly supplied to order.[23]

The Booth copies are made of earthenware and should not deceive even the most inexperienced collector, but at Coalport, the original Caughley plates were re-used with the mark of an open crescent, rather than the expectable Caughley 'C'. Thus, it should be remembered that Worcester only used a hatched crescent on its printed floral patterns. These nineteenth-century 'fakes' – and they can only be described as such – are in a bone china body which has a very strong white translucence and are printed in a particularly harsh blue colour, so should be detected with a degree of care. However, one remains amazed at how frequently these Coalport fakes appear in both the salerooms and antique shops and are passed off, innocently or otherwise, as authentic eighteenth-century Worcester.

References

1 Valentine Green, *History and Antiquities of the City and Suburbs of Worcester*, 1795.
2 *Transactions of the English Ceramic Circle*, Volume 1, Number 1, 1928, p. 20.
3 R. L. Hobson, *Worcester Porcelain*, see Bibliography.
4 See Chapter 2, p. 31.
5 R. W. Binns, *A Century of Potting in the City of Worcester*, see Bibliography.
6 E. J. Climenson, editor, *Passages from the Diaries of Mrs Philip Lybbe Powys, 1756–1808*, 1899, pp. 125 and 126.
7 Geoffrey Wills, 'Worcester Blue and White Porcelain in the Jenkins Collection', *Connoisseur*, December 1954.
8 Previously only Lund's Bristol porcelain had been offered at Castle Green.
9 F. S. Mackenna, *Worcester Porcelain*, see Bibliography.
10 *The Complete Works of Benjamin Franklin*, New York, 1887, Volume III, p. 6.
11 *The Oxford Journal*, quoted by R. W. Binns, *op. cit.*, p. 73, and F. S. Mackenna, *op. cit.*, p. 50.
12 J. E. Nightingale, *Contributions towards the History of English Porcelain*, 1881.
13 Nightingale, *op. cit.*
14 W. M. Binns, *The First Century of English Porcelain*, see Bibliography.
15 R. W. Binns, *op. cit.*
16 R. W. Binns, *op. cit.*
17 Henry Sandon, *The Illustrated Guide to Worcester Porcelain 1751–1793*, see Bibliography.
18 Geoffrey A. Godden, *Caughley and Worcester Porcelains 1775–1800*, see Bibliography.
19 Order Books, Invoices, etc. of Chamberlain & Co., 1788–1795, Library of the Dyson Perrins Museum.
20 Henry Sandon, *Flight and Barr Worcester Porcelain*, see Bibliography.
21 Henry Sandon, *Worcester Porcelain 1751–1793*, *op. cit.*
22 Geoffrey A. Godden, see Bibliography.
23 R. W. Binns, *op. cit.*

Chapter 2

How Blue and White Porcelain Was Made

Since much of the descriptive material in the sections which follow refers to some aspect or other of the actual production technique used in the eighteenth-century Worcester manufacturing process, it might be well at this juncture to have a brief word about how these wares were made.

As we have said, the term 'blue and white' has been used here to describe porcelain which was decorated by either painting or printing with cobalt oxide on a piece of biscuit ware *before* glazing. The colour, then, is beneath the glaze and is protected by it from excessive wear, allowing the porcelain to be used as everyday table china rather than being preserved for special occasions.

The body of Worcester porcelain is sometimes described as 'soft paste'. This somewhat misleading term does not imply that it was any 'softer' than other porcelains, but rather that it belongs to a particular family of porcelains developed in Europe to imitate the original Oriental 'hard paste' body. It is really not possible to describe adequately how one distinguishes between 'hard paste' and 'soft paste' wares, for that is a skill which can only be acquired by handling examples of each type of body over a long period of time. If we can generalise, the hard paste porcelains are more often glassy and cold to the touch when compared to the warmer and somehow more granular quality of soft paste. However, there are about as many exceptions as there are rules here, and we can only encourage you to learn through experience.

All hard paste porcelains, whether Oriental or European, adhere to the classic formula of 'kaolin and petuntse' – china clay and china rock – whereas soft paste bodies can be made from a number of differing recipes. Worcester's version included steatite (Cornish soapstone), and had the advantage of lower firing temperatures than its Continental and Oriental rivals. It produced a body that was easily formed, strong, and not temperamental in firing, resulting in far less kiln breakage than was experienced by its competitors.

Worcester formed this paste into shaped pieces in one of three ways. The most common and well known of these is the 'throwing and turning' process. 'Throwing' is the traditional way of making most objects which are round in section, and consists of centring the clay on the potter's wheel, raising it by hand as the wheel revolves, and shaping it into the desired form, be it teapot, bowl, cup, bottle or mug. When completed, the piece is removed from the wheel with a cutting wire and dried to what was called a 'leather hardness' before being taken to the 'turner'. This particularly skilled craftsman mounted the piece on a hand- or foot-driven lathe, and with the use of a variety of tools removed the surplus clay, shaped the footring, and skimmed the outside surface to its characteristic smoothness.

The second method, 'press-moulding', was used for all pieces, apart from cups, saucers, bowls and plates, which have relief-modelled decoration. Flatware pieces such as spoon trays or leaf or junket dishes were made by pressing a flat 'bat' of clay over a 'hump mould' made of plaster. The mould formed the modelling on the upper surface of the piece while the potter smoothed the back surface with a sponge and water, adding a footring by hand where necessary. Whereas flatware is pressed *over* a convex mould which forms the inner surface of the piece, hollow-ware is made by pressing the clay *into* a concave mould which provides the modelling required on the exterior surface. Frequently, as in the case of sauceboats or teapots, several sections of mould will be required. Here, each section will have its clay bat pressed into its modelled surface separately and then the sections will be joined together so that the entire piece can be assembled. When the moulds are removed, the surplus clay is cleaned from the piece and spouts, knobs and handles are added as required.

The third method of production, which is called 'jolleying', is really a combination of the first two processes, that is, 'throwing' and 'press-moulding'. Like the former, it can only be used to make round shapes, but, like the latter, it provides a method of achieving a modelled surface. It was used to produce all reeded, fluted or chrysanthemum modelled surfaces on cups, saucers, and bowls. As with press-moulding, flatware shapes were made over a hump mould but in this case, mounted on a potter's wheel-head. The clay bat was placed over the mould, and, as the wheel revolved, the potter would press the clay onto the mould with the usual sponge and water; using a hand tool called a 'profile', he would then form the back of the flatware shape, including the footring. For cups and bowls, the process was similar to that used for flatware, except here the mould was hollow (concave) and a flat bat of clay would have a tendency to crease upon introduction into such a surface. Therefore, it was necessary to make a small and roughly thrown 'liner' from clay for use in place of the usual clay bat. With the potter's wheel turning, the craftsman would press this liner against the hollow surface of the mould, again using his sponge and water, and with a wooden, slate, or ceramic profile would smooth the inner part of the round object to the desired shape. It will be seen that jolleying is, in effect, a mechanical 'throwing', with the mould taking the place of the right, or outside hand, and the profile tool used

instead of the left, or inside hand. It is an eighteenth-century method that has formed the basis for all of the sophisticated techniques of ceramic making that are current today.

It is not entirely clear how such plain surfaced objects as saucers or plates were made. It is possible, of course, that they could have been formed by jolleying, using a plain mould to shape the exterior surface while the bottom side was finished by the thrower and his tools as the piece revolved on the wheel. However, we think it more probable that these flatware pieces were made through the normal throwing process to achieve the desired roundness, but it was left to the turner's skill to take away the surplus clay and to actually shape both sides of the flatware piece to the precise delineations required.

In other factories, the further method of 'slip casting' was also used. This process, which was used as an alternative to press-moulding, involved liquid clay, or 'slip', being poured into a porous plaster mould; this was allowed to deposit an even coat of clay all over the inside of the mould before the surplus slip was poured off. The piece would then be allowed to dry, would be removed from the mould and finished as with the press-moulded objects. It was, however, a method fraught with difficulties because of the high shrinkage and potential distortion and did not become properly viable until the technological advances that were made at the end of the following century provided a method of drastically reducing the shrinkage levels. Worcester did use this method during the eighteenth century, but only occasionally, and existing examples of slip-cast ware are extremely rare.

After these various processes had been finished and the pieces had been dried, they would be placed in the biscuit kilns which were sealed and then coal-fired to a temperature of about 1100°C. This firing not only converted the potting mixture into a fused and vitrified biscuit body, but also resulted in a shrinkage of the size of the pieces by about one-sixth as the liquid content of the clay evaporated in the heat of the kiln. Much of the factory wastage occurred at this time, since the shrinkage of the objects was one of the primary causes of cracking and breaking. When the kiln cooled, the biscuit shapes were removed, some being delivered to the decorators to be painted or printed in the underglaze blue colour, the rest sent to be dipped in glaze and returned to the glazing, or 'glost' kiln for further firing and later onglaze decoration.

Blue and white decoration was achieved by one of two methods. Until the 1770s, as has been explained previously, the majority of the Worcester ware was decorated by painting, each item done by an individual painter or group of painters copying from a standard for each pattern. This resulted, or was intended to result in a general adherence to the layout of detail, or 'arrangement' of the pattern, but there would still be differences in the 'treatment' or interpretation of the design by each individual craftsman. The blue colouring used to paint the design was derived from a mixture of cobalt oxides called either 'zaffre' or 'smalt', the latter being a more refined and lighter version of the first. These materials were usually imported from Saxony in more or less finished form, although, in the later part of the century, some cobalt oxides were being refined in England as well. The painting medium was mixed with either water or a variety of oils, according to the painter's own preferences, and applied to the biscuit surface resulting in a brown or blackish design which would only acquire its characteristic blue colouration after the later glost firing in the kiln.

The other method of decoration, of course, was transfer-printing, a process orginally intended for use in onglaze decoration, but quickly adapted for the underglaze blue designs as well. The printing technique was based on a copper plate which had either been etched, or in later years, engraved with the intended design. Coloured oxide mixed with the printing medium was applied to this heated copper plate, and then carefully cleaned from its flat surface, leaving only the etched or engraved lines with colour. A tissue transfer paper wetted with soft soap was placed on the copper plate, rolled through a press, and then peeled off. This transfer paper with its colour print was applied, face down, onto the piece to be decorated and rubbed down firmly, the colour adhering to the biscuit surface. Afterwards the tissue would be washed away, leaving the decoration intact. This technique, with only minor modifications, is essentially the same as that used today, and, as we have already pointed out, had obvious commercial attractions when compared to the slower hand-painted processes.

After the piece had been decorated, it was placed for firing in a cool part of the glost kiln. This allowed the decoration to 'harden on', or fuse to the surface of the piece before being glazed, and avoided much of the running or blurring of the underglaze decoration which is so prevalent in the products of many of Worcester's contemporary competitors. When the pieces had been removed from the 'hardening on' area of the glost kiln, they were cooled and dipped in the lead-based glaze, either by hand or with the use of a wire hanger. To lessen the risk of the glaze fusing the piece to its support or stand while in the glazing kiln, the surplus glaze would usually be wiped away from the lower part of the piece and the inside of the footring, leaving a glaze free margin where this had been done. The pieces were then taken to the glost kiln for their final firing, thus completing the manufacturing process.

Chapter 3

An Introduction to the Worcester Patterns

The patterns which follow are not intended to represent a comprehensive encyclopaedia of every blue and white design utilized by the Worcester factory during the 1751–90 period covered by this book. Indeed, as stated previously, we know for a fact that there were numerous patterns which have not been included, as 'wasters' of both biscuit and glost ware have been found during the several excavations of the original Worcester factory site which contain incomplete fragments of patterns not illustrated here. Doubtless, too, many collectors and dealers have pieces of Worcester blue and white which bear patterns that we have not seen. But the patterns which have been included, we believe, comprise all of those contained in the major museums in Britain, and in all of the major private collections to which we have been given access. Further, we have gone back through the sale catalogues of the leading auction houses over the past two decades, and have included any unique patterns found in those sales, provided always that we could be reasonably sure from the evidence available to us that the piece sold was authentically Worcester. To the extent possible, we have relied on the findings of the various excavations of the Warmstry House factory site to authenticate our work, believing, as do most authorities, that if a biscuit waster has been uncovered during those excavations which bears a pattern also found on a completed piece, proof of a Worcester origin for that pattern can be assured. Nevertheless, we must repeat that this work cannot be taken as all inclusive, and our reader must not assume that an example is not a Worcester piece simply because he cannot find an identical or similar pattern here.

It should also be remembered that the hand-painted patterns often vary considerably from one example to another, and that these variations can easily mislead one into believing that the piece has a unique pattern which has not been pictured in this book. Some of the most popular patterns were used for several decades at the factory, and were painted by dozens of artists during that time, each of whom may have lent a minor or even substantial distinction to it. Further, both the style and the care with which the pieces were painted tended to change over time, often to such an extent that it was difficult for us to agree amongst ourselves that the essential elements of the pattern were still preserved by the later work. Where this occurs with respect to a particular pattern, we have noted it in the comments following the illustration. We can only advise the reader to study the pattern carefully, observe the elements of its composition and their location on the piece in question, and then compare these with the example herein always bearing in mind that patterns, whether painted or printed, were necessarily amended, restricted, or expanded to adapt to the available space on the piece being decorated.

The Arrangement of Patterns

The patterns have been organized in the book in a manner which we hope will facilitate identification, rather than in any scientific or historical sequence. First, we have divided the patterns into two principal groups, I, The Painted Patterns and II, The Printed Patterns, so we must remind the reader as to how one can distinguish the differences between the two methods of decoration. A painted pattern, of course, was applied with a hand-held brush, whereas the printed pattern follows an etched or engraved line in a copper plate. Thus, the first examination should be towards any area in the pattern where shading or solid colour has been represented. In most instances, a brush cannot match the precision of an etched or engraved line, thus the 'hatching' on leaves, rocks, etc. in the pattern will either tend to be more inexact and somewhat more obvious than in the printed pattern, or, alternatively, will be accomplished through the 'washing' of solid colour. This can best be understood by comparing the two following illustrations of a prunus flower, the left one being painted and the right one printed:

A printing technique can never supply areas of 'washed' colour, that is, a shading of colouration which can only be accomplished by brushwork. Rather, the printed version must duplicate this shading technique by cross-hatching or by a series of narrow lines which, when viewed from a distance, accomplish the same purpose. Observe below the illustration of a rock and its reflection in water as seen in a painted pattern (the left example) as compared with the printed version on the right:

It should be noted that there were a very few later printed designs which had 'washed' colours added by hand after the print had been applied to the piece, but these examples have been noted in the text.

Once it has been determined whether the pattern was painted or printed, the location of the pattern within the appropriate section can be approximated according to the following classification of the subsections which we have used.

I.   The Painted Patterns

A. *Prominent Figures.*   Where a pattern embodies a representation of a person whose facial features such as eyes, nose or mouth can be clearly seen, the pattern will be found in this subsection, regardless of whether the pattern contains other characteristics such as bird, animal or landscape background.

B. *Other Figures.*   These are patterns which contain a human figure painted with no discernable facial features, usually placed in a garden or other landscape.

C. *Birds and Animals.*   If the pattern does not portray a human figure, but does picture a bird or other creature, even as a minor aspect of the pattern, the design will be found in this subsection. The only exception to this is made in the case of 'squiggles', that is, distant flying birds done with a single brush stroke in the pattern background.

D. *Landscapes.*   These patterns represent a garden or landscape scene which is painted with no figure, bird or animal included.

E. *Floral and Fruit.*   As the title implies, these patterns are of flowers, foliage, and/or fruit, not set in a garden or landscape background.

F. *Formal Patterns.*   These are the patterns that do not fall into any of the other categories, and display a formalistic design as opposed to the portrayal of a human, animal or natural setting or object.

II. The Printed Patterns

The classification of the printed pattern sub-sections follows that used for the painted patterns, except where noted below:

A. *Prominent Figures.*

B. *Landscapes, Birds and Animals.* Because of the relatively small number of patterns involved, we have combined all landscapes, bird or animal patterns into this category, whether or not any of these include a figure without prominent features. Thus, this subsection encompasses in one category that included in subsections B, C, and D of the painted designs.

C. *Floral and Fruit.*

In both the painted and printed subsections, we have tried to organize the patterns so as to show the development of a type of design, or to group patterns which obviously are related to each other or are derived from a common pattern root. If a printed pattern has a clear relationship with a painted original, we have had to be content to note this in the comments under each.

Pattern Information

Where possible or useful, we have illustrated the painted pattern design with a tone drawing as well as with the usual photograph or photographs. The drawings are intended to show what the camera cannot, the arrangement of the pattern right around a shape. The method is to display the pattern as if it had been unwound from the pot and laid down flat, rather like a schoolroom map of the world. The drawings have been done in a manner which approaches the original painting as closely as possible in style, method and sequence of execution, and the only liberty taken with what were otherwise careful copies was an occasional attempt to clarify the design where it appeared ambiguous on the original.

To accompany the photographs and drawings of the patterns, we have included some textual information with regard to each of these which we hope will prove useful. This information follows the format below:

(a) *Date Range.* Within a degree of tolerable error, the dates during which a pattern was utilized at Worcester can be determined on the basis of a number of factors. The most important clue as to the first date of utilization, as explained earlier, is derived from the information gained through the several excavations of the original factory site. Further insight can be had from examination of the surviving examples of pieces bearing the pattern, as the shape of the piece, the style of painting used, the presence or absence of factory marks, as well as the tone of the cobalt colour, can be useful guides to the approximate date of manufacture of any particular piece. It must be recognized, nevertheless, that establishing a date range is not an exact science, and variations and exceptions will undoubtedly occur.

(b) *Rarity.* We have based our judgement of rarity on a number of factors, including the frequency with which we have seen pieces bearing the particular pattern, either offered in the major auction house sales or within the stock of the better known antique shops, or as items in the numerous public and private collections we have examined. The reader should note that 'rarity' is not necessarily synonymous with 'expensiveness', which appears to be more closely related to the overall desirability of the pattern and of the piece upon which it is used than on uniqueness alone. Our evaluation ranges from those 'very rare' patterns where only a single example or at most a handful of pieces are known to exist, through 'rare', 'uncommon', 'not uncommon', and finally 'common' patterns where examples can usually be found on the shelves of most of the dealers specializing in the sale of antique English porcelains.

(c) *Border Numbers.* At the end of the book (III, The Border Patterns), we show the borders which most commonly accompany a design pattern, and, while we have tried to be as inclusive as possible, there will always be those examples that we have missed. The painted borders are listed numerically from 1 to 127, while the printed patterns are listed alphabetically from A to U, and their number or letter in the border section will correspond to its equivalent listed with the pattern itself.

(d) *Marks.*   To some degree, the kind of mark which is likely to be found on a piece decorated with a particular pattern can be predetermined by the date range during which the pattern was produced. On painted patterns made before roughly 1760, there is likely to be some kind of workman's mark, if any mark at all, and there will usually be an open crescent thereafter. On printed ware, you may find an open crescent on the rare and early pieces, and invariably after about 1760 the mark will be a hatched crescent, followed by the series of disguised numerals from about 1780 onwards on certain patterns. Nevertheless, there are variations from these norms, so we have indicated what kind of mark is most likely to be found on a particular pattern. Where a pattern is usually or always accompanied by its own unique mark, this will be illustrated, along with the photograph or drawing of the design. We have regretfully but deliberately omitted reproducing any catalogue of workmen's marks for two very good reasons. Firstly we have no comprehensive record of the dozens of marks and the many variations of these which appear on the early Worcester ware, and an illustration of only a sampling of these, we fear, would produce more confusion than benefit. Secondly, we freely admit having no really authoritative theory as to what these workmen's marks actually signify, and, until the pressing need for further research in this area is satisfied, would much prefer to avoid the controversy that would follow from offering basically unknowledgeable views as to their meaning and importance.

(e) *Shapes Used.*   Here we have tried to pinpoint the probable kinds of wares upon which the pattern is most likely to be found, either generically (that is, by reference to the method of manufacture, such as 'thrown and turned', 'press-moulded' etc.), by category ('teaware' or 'dessertware'), or by specific shape and perhaps dimension ('a press-moulded sauceboat, 6 in. in length'). As explained earlier, a complete tea and coffee service numbered forty-three pieces, and included in addition to the basic teawares a coffee pot and cover, tea canister and cover, and a spoon tray. Thus, a reference to 'teawares' will encompass all of the shapes normally found in the standard tea and coffee service. We also refer occasionally to 'dessertware'. A dessert service would usually comprise two tureens, their covers and stands, sometimes accompanied by a sugar ladle, sixteen shaped dishes, either shell-shaped, heart-shaped (sometimes called 'kidney-shaped'), square or oval, generally in combinations of two or four of each, and a set of dessert plates supplied in multiples of twelve, eighteen, or twenty-four, as the customer desired. Both the tea services and the dessert services could be supplemented by the addition of other pieces, but we have tried to identify these separately, where useful.

(f) *Commentary.*   Finally, we have tried to give whatever further information we feel might be useful in understanding the pattern or how it can be best identified or verified. Where wasters decorated with the design have been found in the excavations, we have said so, and, in the case of the less usual patterns, have indicated where examples might be found in the major public collections or illustrated in other books on English porcelains. We have also tried to comment on the variations expectable in the way the details of the pattern have been arranged, or on the variations which can be found in the treatment of the subject matter by different painters over a period of use. More importantly, we have also tried to point to the source of the design or to other patterns to which the design may be linked or from which it has evolved, and, in this way, demonstrate how a piece of Worcester origin can be identified as well by the style and quality of its painting and its subject matter as by the other characteristics of the piece itself.

Before turning to the illustrations of the patterns themselves, there is one final matter that should be called to the reader's attention: the names which have been given to each of the patterns. With very few exceptions, the Warmstry House factory did not ascribe particular titles to the designs that were employed in the 1751–90 period, and, of the few names used then, even fewer have survived into common usage today. Over the years, dealers and collectors have associated a dozen or so of the patterns included here with a particular descriptive title – for example, 'Pine Cone', 'Mansfield', 'Peony', 'Cannonball', etc. – but the fact remains that the vast majority of the Worcester designs have no commonly accepted names, and therefore those given here are primarily of our own invention and are intended only as an aid to identification.

THE PATTERNS

I. The Painted Patterns

A. Prominent Figures

1 The Primitive Chinaman
2 The Lady with a Stormcloud
3 The Willow Root
4 The Lange Lijzen
5 The Writhing Rock
6 The Waiting Chinaman
7 The Arcade
8 The Telephone Box
9 The Storyteller
10 The Chinese Garden
11 The Tureen Panel Group
12 The Island Shrine
13 The Gardener
14 The Cracked Ice Ground
15 The Floral Reserve
16 The Arabesque Reserve
17 The Walk in the Garden
18 The Tambourine
19 The Children at Play
20 The Eloping Bride
21 The Brigand
22 The Three-Dot Painter Jug
23 The Acrobats/The Beckoning Chinaman
24 The Man with a Lunchbox
25 The Man with a Parasol
26 The Umbrella Man
27 The Lonely Chinaman
28 The Chinaman and Fence
29 The Strolling Chinaman
30 The Fisherman with a Net
31 The Man with a Bomb
32 The Willow Bridge Fisherman
33 The Captive Bird
34 St George and the Dragon

The Primitive Chinaman

DATE RANGE: 1751–1753

RARITY: Very rare

BORDER NOS: 71

MARKS: Workmen's marks, if any

SHAPES USED: Plain thrown and turned shapes, including a small coffee pot or chocolate pot, as illustrated, a coffee cup, $2\frac{5}{8}$ in. high, and a bowl, $4\frac{1}{2}$ in. diameter.

COMMENTARY: We are aware of only three examples of this pattern, as mentioned in the description of the shapes used. The bowl is owned by the Castle Museum in Norwich, and Dr Watney illustrates the coffee cup from his own collection (Plate 26B).† During the excavations of the original Worcester factory site, both a biscuit and a glost fragment of the border pattern were found, and, as the border is unique to this pattern, this may be considered as persuasive evidence of its Worcester origin.

Coffee Pot (lacking cover), 5 in. high (Victoria and Albert Museum)*

Bowl
Complete pattern

*Unless otherwise indicated, pieces illustrated are in the collections stated in the captions.
†For all literature quoted full reference is given in the Bibliography, page 364.

The Lady with a Stormcloud

DATE RANGE: 1751–1753

RARITY: Very rare

BORDER NOS: None

MARKS: None

SHAPES USED: A press-moulded, lobed coffee cup, $2\frac{5}{8}$ in. high, with elaborately modelled handle.

COMMENTARY: The coffee cup pictured is the only known example of the pattern. An undecorated biscuit waster of an identically shaped cup was found in the factory site excavations. Both Sandon (Plate 15), and Watney (Plate 23A) have illustrated the pattern.

Coffee Cup, $2\frac{5}{8}$ in. high
(Dyson Perrins Museum)

Coffee Cup
Complete pattern

The Willow Root

DATE RANGE: 1751–1755

RARITY: Uncommon

BORDER NOS: None

MARKS: Workmen's marks

SHAPES USED: Plain thrown and turned shapes, including spreading base and bell-shaped mugs, spreading base coffee cans, jugs, and bowls of various sizes.

COMMENTARY: This is one of the few patterns of Worcester manufacture where the identical design was used on both blue and white and polychrome decorated

Mug, 3¾ in high
(Dyson Perrins Museum)

ware. In the blue and white version, a very considerable variation will be found in both the treatment and the arrangement of the design, some examples even eliminating the central figure altogether, as indicated by the tone drawing of the coffee can, and others indicating the foliage through cross-hatching rather than the normally careful naturalistic painting style. A number of both biscuit and glost fragments with the pattern were found in the excavations at the factory site, and completed examples of the design can be seen at both the Dyson Perrins and Victoria and Albert Museums.

Mug
Complete pattern
Coffee Can
Pattern variation

Left: *Gugglet, 10 in. high
(Private Collection)*
Right: *Reverse pattern*

DATE RANGE: 1753–1755

RARITY: Very rare

BORDER NOS: 83

MARKS: Workmen's marks

SHAPES USED: Plain thrown and turned gugglets or bottles, usually around 10 in. high.

COMMENTARY: The very close connection between this pattern and the design used in 'The Willow Root' and 'The Writhing Rock' (Patterns I.A.3 and 5) should be noted, each only differing sufficiently in its arrangement of the details and the position of the central figure to suggest that it constitutes a separate although closely linked pattern. Watney (Plate 27C) and Barrett (Plate 42) both illustrate examples, and there are gugglets decorated with this pattern in the collections of the City of Birmingham Museum and Art Gallery and the Bristol City Art Gallery, where a piece is on loan.

The Writhing Rock

DATE RANGE: 1753–1755

RARITY: Very rare

BORDER NOS: 82

MARKS: A three character, pseudo-Chinese mark, as illustrated.

SHAPES USED: Plain rimmed plates, either 9 in. or 9¼ in. in diameter.

COMMENTARY: The very few known examples of this pattern display little variation in either the painting style employed or in the arrangement of the design. As noted, there are strong links between this pattern and 'The Lange Lijzen' (Pattern I.A.4) which precedes. There are two examples of these plates in the Dyson Perrins Museum. Another was sold at Sotheby's on 28 April 1970 (Lot 69) as part of the Jenkins Collection.

Plate, 9 in. diameter
(Sotheby Parke Bernet and Co.)

Mark

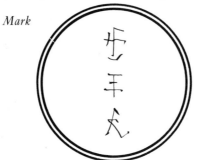

The Waiting Chinaman

DATE RANGE: 1765–1775

RARITY: Not uncommon

BORDER NOS: 8

MARKS: Open crescent or script 'W'

SHAPES USED: Plain thrown and turned tewares of the usual range.

COMMENTARY: Worcester also did a version of this pattern with a headless figure in underglaze blue using onglaze polychrome additions to complete the design. The pattern differs very little in either treatment or arrangement over the decade of its use, with almost all of the examples being neatly and precisely painted, albeit by perceptibly different hands. Caughley used this pattern, also in painted underglaze blue, around 1775 and its version is identical in almost every respect to the Worcester pattern. This can be easily confused, particularly when found in conjunction with Caughley's painted 'C' mark. Both biscuit and glost fragments of the design were found in the factory site excavations, one of which is illustrated by Sandon (Plate 86).

Left: *Bowl, 6⅛ in. diameter (Authors' Collections)*
Above: *Saucer*
Complete pattern

DATE RANGE: 1765–1770

RARITY: Uncommon

BORDER NOS: 44

MARKS: A pseudo-Chinese symbol, as illustrated.

SHAPES USED: A limited range of plain thrown and turned teawares.

COMMENTARY: The pattern is taken directly from a K'ang Hsi design, and the Worcester version shows little variation in either its treatment or in the arrangement of its detail. Watney illustrates another teabowl and saucer (Plate 35B), and Hobson illustrates a saucer similar to that illustrated here (Plate XXI, bottom left).

Saucer, $4\frac{1}{8}$ in. diameter
(Dyson Perrins Museum)

Teabowl
Complete pattern

Mark

The Telephone Box

DATE RANGE: *c.* 1770

RARITY: Not uncommon

BORDER NOS: 28

MARKS: Open crescent

SHAPES USED: Thrown and turned garniture sets, usually of five pieces, which will include some combination of spill vases ($7\frac{3}{4}$ in. to $9\frac{1}{2}$ in. high) and covered vases (8 in. to 12 in. high).

COMMENTARY: This is another of the very limited number of Worcester underglaze blue patterns which also appear exactly on polychrome-decorated pieces. The carefully painted designs comprise four groups of figures, including two single figures and two pairs. Usually, the single figures are used on the smaller spill vases, and the pairs are found on the larger pieces. A biscuit fragment of the pattern used on the vase covers was found in the excavation of the Worcester factory site.

Vases with Covers, 12 in. high
Beaker Vases, $9\frac{1}{2}$ in. high
(Sotheby Parke Bernet and Co.)

Vase with Cover
Detail

The Storyteller

Tureen Stand, 18¼ in. long (British Museum)

DATE RANGE: 1755–1758

RARITY: Very rare

BORDER NOS: None

MARKS: Workmen's marks

SHAPES USED: A press-moulded, heavily modelled tureen stand, about 18½ in. long.

COMMENTARY: The tureen stand illustrated is shown in Watney's book (Plate 30A). See the next pattern, 'The Chinese Garden' (Pattern I.A.10) for an identically shaped tureen stand decorated with a related but distinguishable design.

Tureen Stand, 18¼ in. long (Sotheby Parke Bernet and Co.)

DATE RANGE: 1755–1758

RARITY: Very rare

BORDER NOS: None

MARKS: Workmen's marks

SHAPES USED: Press-moulded, heavily modelled tureen stands, 18¼ in. in length.

COMMENTARY: An identical shape is also found in 'The Storyteller' tureen stand (Pattern I.A.9) opposite. This, together with the style of painting utilized, strongly supports its Worcester origin. The stand illustrated was sold by Sotheby's in its 7 October 1969 sale as Lot 139. Another identical stand is owned by a private collector in the United States. The floral sprays which appear along the border area are very similar, but not identical, to those that appear on 'The Butterboat Floral' (Pattern I.E.38).

The Tureen Panel Group

DATE RANGE: 1753–1755

RARITY: Very rare

BORDER NOS: 80 on one of known examples.

MARKS: Workmen's marks

SHAPES USED: Large press-moulded and heavily modelled tureens and covers with modelled handles and dolphin-moulded finials, usually around $17\frac{1}{2}$ in. long and about $8\frac{1}{2}$ in. high to the top of the cover. The Victoria and Albert tureen cover is the only one of these that has a twig finial, rather than the usual dolphin.

COMMENTARY: There are at least four of these tureens and covers each decorated with what seem to be different, although

Top: *Tureen and Cover, $17\frac{1}{2}$ in. long*
(Dyson Perrins Museum)

Centre: *Reverse pattern*

Below: *Interior of Tureen*

related, groups of designs. Of the two other examples we know but have not shown here, one is in the Victoria and Albert Museum, and the other was illustrated by Barrett (Plate 43). The group comprises a range of chinoiserie subjects painted within the panels of the four examples, and as far as we know each is entirely different from any other to be found in the group, although it is possible that on examples other than those mentioned above, there may be some interchangeable use of them. The tureens sat on large modelled stands such as those decorated with 'The Chinese Garden' and 'The Storyteller' (Patterns I.A.9 and 10) to which they have an obvious link in use if not in actual painting style. The original mould for the tureens is still in existence at the Dyson Perrins Museum.

Top: *Tureen and Cover, 17½in. long*
(Rous (Lench Collection)

Centre: *Reverse pattern*

Below: *Interior of Tureen*

*Basket, 15½ in. long
(Victoria and Albert Museum)*

DATE RANGE: 1755–1757

RARITY: Very rare

BORDER NOS: It has its own unique border, as seen in the photograph, along with variations of 18 and 116.

MARKS: Workmen's marks

SHAPES USED: An oval press-moulded basket with trellis-moulded piercedwork, 15½ in. long.

COMMENTARY: This pattern is distinguished more because of the very unusual shape upon which it appears than because of the design itself which contains many of the familiar details used so frequently on Worcester chinoiserie decorations of this period. A careful and detailed examination of the figure standing within the island shrine itself will reveal facial features, hence its inclusion within this section rather than in section I.B.

following, where this design would integrate more easily. See for example, 'The Six-Piered Bridge' (Pattern I.B.33) or 'The Picture Scroll Landscape' (Pattern I.B.24). The only known example is that illustrated above.

The Gardener

Mug, 5⅞ in. high
(Authors' Collections)

DATE RANGE: 1765–1775

RARITY: Uncommon

BORDER NOS: Usually none; rarely, 2 and 52

MARKS: Open crescent

SHAPES USED: A range of plain thrown and turned shapes, including a variety of sizes of cylinder and bell-shaped mugs, coffee cups, saucers, and sparrowbeak jugs.

COMMENTARY: The painting of this pattern is unusual in that a darker colour of cobalt has been used on top of a lighter undercolour in the clothing of the two figures. The design shows little variation from example to example, except that required to adapt the arrangement to the shape of the piece. Both biscuit and glost wasters decorated with the pattern were found in the excavations of the factory site, one of which is illustrated by Sandon (Plate 103), along with a completed example. Many of the major public porcelain collections, including the Dyson Perrins and Victoria and Albert Museums, have pieces decorated with this design.

Teabowl
Complete pattern

Right: *Mug, 6 in. high
(Dyson Perrins Museum)*
Far right: *Reverse pattern*

Below: *Mug
Complete pattern*

DATE RANGE: 1765–1775

RARITY: Uncommon

BORDER NOS: None

MARKS: Open crescent

SHAPES USED: Plain thrown and turned mugs, both cylinder and bell-shaped, in a variety of sizes from $3\frac{1}{2}$ in. to 6 in. in height.

COMMENTARY: It should be noted, in comparing the photographs of the bell-shaped mug with the tone drawing of the cylinder mug, that while the central figure appears consistently in all examples, the background arrangement and content can differ widely. In keeping with other derivative designs, the pattern was well painted, with considerable care being taken in its execution. There is an obvious relationship to the designs of the two patterns that follow (Patterns I.A.15 and 16). Biscuit and glost fragments of the pattern were found in the factory site excavations, and examples of completed pieces can be seen at the Victoria and Albert Museum as well as at the Dyson Perrins Museum.

54

The Floral Reserve

DATE RANGE: *c.* 1770

RARITY: Very rare

BORDER NOS: 1

MARKS: Open crescent

SHAPES USED: A plain thrown and turned cylinder mug, $4\frac{3}{4}$ in. high.

COMMENTARY: The only known example of this pattern is on the cylinder mug illustrated. It has an obviously close stylistic connection to the preceding pattern, 'The Cracked Ice Ground' (Pattern I.A.14), whose authenticity was established by the factory excavations. The figure that is used as the central detail here is almost identical to that on the pattern preceding and has a similar relationship to that on 'The Arabesque Reserve' (Pattern I.A.16) which follows.

Mug, $4\frac{3}{4}$ in. high
(Gilbert Bradley Collection)

The Arabesque Reserve

Teapot and Cover, 5 in. high
(Castle Museum, Norwich)

Teapot detail

DATE RANGE: *c.* 1770

RARITY: Very rare

BORDER NOS: 46

MARKS: Open crescent, if any

SHAPES USED: Plain thrown and turned teawares, including a teapot and cover, 5 in. high, as illustrated, and a teabowl and saucer of the usual size.

COMMENTARY: A biscuit fragment was found in the course of an early excavation at the Worcester factory site which was decorated with both a part of the reserve and one of the figures featuring in this design, so its origin can be assumed. The teabowl and saucer was included in the 1979 Albert Amor Ltd Exhibition of Blue and White 18th Century English Soft Paste Porcelain, Catalogue Number 43. The figure seated to the left of the design, atop the 'pile of doughnuts' rock, has a marked similarity to that on the reverse pattern of 'The Cracked Ice Ground' (Pattern I.A.14). On the Castle Museum teapot the same pattern is repeated on the reverse side, although it would seem possible that, on other yet unseen examples, the primary pattern of 'The Cracked Ice Ground' could have been used here as well.

The Walk in the Garden

DATE RANGE: 1755–1765

RARITY: Not uncommon

BORDER NOS: Usually none; rarely, 62

MARKS: Workmen's marks on the earlier examples, open crescents thereafter.

SHAPES USED: Plain thrown and turned shapes, the most common being cylinder and bell-shaped mugs ranging from $3\frac{1}{4}$ in. to 6 in. in height. The pattern is also found on spreading base mugs, large sparrowbeak jugs, teapots, teabowls, saucers, and various coffee cups.

COMMENTARY: Some minor variations in the arrangement and treatment of the pattern will be found on different pieces, primarily due to the shapes and sizes of the wares decorated. The usual variation is the omission of the large tree on the smaller shapes. There were a number of biscuit and glost fragments found in the factory site excavations, and several of the larger public collections have completed examples of the design. Derby used this exact pattern, but with an elaborate border.

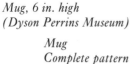

*Mug, 6 in. high
(Dyson Perrins Museum)*

*Mug
Complete pattern*

The Tambourine

DATE RANGE: 1753–1758

RARITY: Uncommon

BORDER NOS: Usually none; rarely, a version of 63

MARKS: Workmen's marks

SHAPES USED: Plain thrown and turned pieces, including the usual range of tewares. It is also found on small flaring base mugs, as illustrated, usually from $4\frac{1}{2}$ in. to 5 in. high.

COMMENTARY: The name of this pattern has been in common use for some years, and we have simply repeated it here, despite the fact that nowhere in the design can one find anything resembling a 'tambourine'. Both biscuit and glost wasters were uncovered by the excavations at the factory site. Spero shows a similar mug on page 30 of his book and Dr Watney illustrates a teapot with the design (Plate 29A). Very little variation is likely to be found in either the treatment or arrangement of this pattern, despite the different shapes upon which it was used.

Saucer
Complete pattern

Below: *Mug, $2\frac{1}{2}$in. high (Private Collection)*
Below right: *Reverse pattern*

The Children at Play

Plate, 9¼ in. diameter
(Godden Reference Collection)

Mark

DATE RANGE: *c.* 1755

RARITY: Very rare

BORDER NOS: 124

MARKS: There are several Chinese-type emblems painted on the back of the wide rim, and a mark on the base, as illustrated.

SHAPES USED: Plain thrown and turned rimmed plates, either 8½ in. or 9¼ in. in diameter, with a countersunk base.

COMMENTARY: A glost fragment of the border pattern, which is unique to this design, was found in the 1979 factory site excavations. Examples of the pattern have been illustrated by Barrett (Plate 44B) and by Geoffrey Godden in his introductory work on blue and white porcelain (Plate 20). Barrett states that the pattern is a direct copy of an original K'ang Hsi design, and, while we cannot confirm this from our own experience, the pattern is certainly akin to the many examples of the 'children at play' (sometimes collectively referred to as 'wa wa' type) paintings used on Oriental porcelain earlier in the eighteenth century.

The Eloping Bride

DATE RANGE: 1765–1770

RARITY: Uncommon

BORDER NOS: 43

MARKS: A pseudo-Chinese mark, as illustrated.

SHAPES USED: Plain thrown and turned teawares of the usual range.

COMMENTARY: This design, which is almost always very finely painted, was based on a Chinese original but has been slightly simplified by the elimination of some of the background usually found on the Oriental pattern. The pattern has been extensively illustrated in previous works on Worcester porcelain, including those of Rissik Marshall (Plate 9 [153]), Barrett (Plate 43B), and Watney (Plate 35D), and examples can be found in several of the major public collections including the Victoria and Albert Museum. A glost fragment decorated with the design was found in the factory site excavations.

Saucer
Complete pattern

Marks under Rim

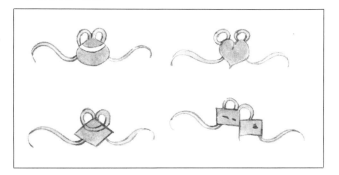

Bowl, 6⅜ in. diameter
(Dyson Perrins Museum)

Mark on Base

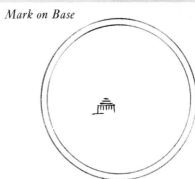

The Brigand

DATE RANGE: 1760–1765

RARITY: Very rare

BORDER NOS: 55 and 59

MARKS: A pseudo-Chinese mark, as illustrated.

SHAPES USED: Plain thrown and turned bowls, ranging from $7\frac{3}{8}$ in. to 8 in. in diameter.

COMMENTARY: The probable inspiration for this design is said to be the Chinese fable of the encounter of Yong Kwei-Fei and Ming Hwang. In the Worcester version, the princess sits within her rickshaw chariot, watching the galloping horseman whose banner, uniquely, flows against the prevailing direction of travel. The scene on the interior of the bowl is believed to be Li T'ai Po, the drunken poet, flanked by his two beloved wine jars. The letters on the horseman's banner appear to have no real significance, although

they have been a topic of some considerable discussion in ceramic circles. The only public collection, to our knowledge, that has an example of this pattern is the British Museum. Watney illustrates a piece (Plate 35A), and another was included in the 1979 Albert Amor Ltd Exhibition, as Catalogue Number 45.

Bowl
Interior pattern

Bowl
Complete pattern

Mark

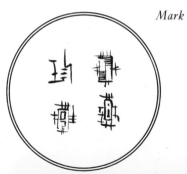

Bowl, 7¼ in. diameter
(Gilbert Bradley Collection)

The Three-Dot Painter Jug

DATE RANGE: *c.* 1751

RARITY: Very rare, perhaps unique

BORDER NOS: A version of 17

MARKS: None

SHAPES USED: A large plain thrown and turned jug.

COMMENTARY: This jug and another similar but distinct piece in the Victoria and Albert Museum are the most elaborate of a group of wares painted by this artist, whose work can be traced through the presence of a number of features always found in his painting, notably the blotchy rendering of the figures, the large-sailed ships, and most noticeably the use of three dot-like rocks arranged in a triangle and frequently repeated on each piece. The craftsman, who is usually referred to as 'the three-dot painter', undoubtedly worked at Lund's factory in Bristol before moving to Worcester, but the shape of this particular piece, the type of paste employed, and the archeological evidence now in hand lead us to believe that this example was produced at Warmstry House in the earliest days of the Worcester factory. The painting is unique and in all probability does not constitute a 'pattern' in the usual sense, but the importance of the piece itself would seem to justify its inclusion here.

Jug, 7⅛ in. high
(Dyson Perrins Museum)

The Acrobats/The Beckoning Chinaman

Top: *Tureen, 11½ in. diameter*
(Private Collection)
Above: *Reverse pattern*

DATE RANGE: 1751–1752

RARITY: Very rare

BORDER NOS: None

MARKS: None

SHAPES USED: A thrown and turned tureen, 11½ in. diameter.

COMMENTARY: The only known example of this pattern is in a private collection in London. It is a most interesting transitional piece between the Lund's Bristol paste and that used by Worcester in its earliest days, the press-moulded handles being made of an entirely different kind of clay than that used in the thrown and turned body. The style of painting, as well as the subject matter depicted, relates closely to that on contemporary polychrome decorated wares, containing ingredients found in several coloured patterns by the same names, 'The Acrobats' and 'The Beckoning Chinaman'. It should be noted, however, that these two designs will not necessarily appear in conjunction with one another in every case, and could well be found separately, or indeed with other patterns of the same date range.

The Man with a Lunchbox

DATE RANGE: 1753–1755

RARITY: Very rare

BORDER NOS: None

MARKS: None

SHAPES USED: A plain thrown and turned punch pot, 8 in. high.

COMMENTARY: A careful examination of this pattern, along with 'The Man with a Parasol' (Pattern I.A.25) that follows, will show that the central figure has been combined with bits and pieces of several other more widely used Worcester designs, including 'The Willow Root' (Pattern I.A.3) and 'The Crescent Moon' (Pattern I.B.4). Possibly the painter of these large pieces, familiar with the more commonly used designs, simply used these to fill in the spaces remaining after the primary feature of the pattern had been drawn. The only other known example of this pattern besides that illustrated here is on another punch pot, in the private Godden Reference Collection in Worthing, which can be viewed by serious collectors by prior arrangement with Mr Geoffrey Godden.

▲ *Punch Pot, 8 in. high, lacking its cover. (Castle Museum, Norwich)*

▼ *Punch Pot*
Complete pattern

The Man with a Parasol

*Punch Pot and Cover, 8 in. high
(Sotheby Parke Bernet and Co.)*

DATE RANGE: 1753–1755

RARITY: Very rare

BORDER NOS: None

MARKS: Workmen's marks

SHAPES USED: A plain thrown and turned punch pot and cover, 8 in. high.

COMMENTARY: The only known example of this pattern is on the punch pot and cover illustrated, sold by Sotheby's as a part of the Jenkins Collection in its 28 April 1970 sale (Lot 40) and now owned by the Godden Reference Collection. The design on the reverse of the punch pot is 'The Man with a Lunchbox' (Pattern I.A.24). As described in the previous pattern, the total design incorporates a number of elements from better known Worcester designs. The handle and knop of the illustrated punch pot and cover are obviously not original, and are probably eighteenth-century turned wood replacements of a different form.

The Umbrella Man

DATE RANGE: 1753–1755

RARITY: Very rare

BORDER NOS: 22 and 55

MARKS: Workmen's marks

SHAPES USED: A plain thrown and turned tureen and cover, 9 in. diameter, with modelled handles and a uniquely shaped twig knop on the cover.

COMMENTARY: The shape of this tureen is as rare as the design used to decorate it. The artistic connection between the pattern and that of 'The Man with a Parasol' (Pattern I.A.25) which precedes it is so close that one could conclude that they are only variations on the same theme. The differences that do exist between them and the rarity of this particular shape, however, lead us to believe that they should be illustrated as separate patterns. The only known example of the pattern is that illustrated here.

Tureen Cover
Complete pattern

Tureen Interior
Complete pattern

Tureen and Cover, 9 in. diameter
(Dyson Perrins Museum)

Tureen
Reverse pattern

The Lonely Chinaman

DATE RANGE: 1753–1755

RARITY: Very rare

BORDER NOS: None

MARKS: Workmen's marks

SHAPES USED: A plain thrown and turned cover for a tureen or large bowl, 9 in. diameter.

COMMENTARY: The only known example of this pattern is on the cover illustrated. The design falls into the stylistic group of painting that encompasses such patterns as 'The Umbrella Man' (Pattern I.A.26) and 'The Man with a Lunchbox' (Pattern I.A.24), although this pattern involves details not previously seen in those.

Tureen Cover, 9 in. diameter (Godden Reference Collection)

The Chinaman and Fence

DATE RANGE: 1756–1758

RARITY: Very rare

BORDER NOS: None

MARKS: Workmen's marks, if any.

SHAPES USED: Plain thrown and turned shapes, including the $5\frac{1}{4}$ in. high sparrowbeak jug illustrated and a $4\frac{3}{4}$ in. high cylinder mug.

COMMENTARY: A cylinder mug decorated with the same pattern as that on the jug illustrated here was included in the 1979 Albert Amor Ltd Exhibition of 18th Century English Blue and White Porcelain, Catalogue Number 11. There appears to be a strong relationship between this pattern and the landscape used on 'The Leaf Dish Fence' (Pattern I.D.14), although the latter lacks the central figure used here.

Cream Jug, $5\frac{1}{4}$ in. high
(Gilbert Bradley Collection)

Cream Jug
Complete pattern

Sauceboat, 6¼ in. long
(Authors' Collections)

DATE RANGE: 1753–1755

RARITY: Very rare

BORDER NOS: 77

MARKS: None

SHAPES USED: A press-moulded, high-footed sauceboat with lobed modelled handle, 6½ in. long.

COMMENTARY: The sauceboat illustrated was purchased at Christie's sale of 23 January 1978 (Lot 303). Another sauceboat with an identical pattern was formerly owned by Simon Spero of China Choice Antiques in London, but its present ownership is unknown. Note the stylistic similarity between the central figure of this design and that found in the previous pattern, 'The Chinaman and Fence' (Pattern I.A.28).

Interior pattern

The Fisherman with a Net

Sauceboat, 7½ in. long
(Authors' Collections)

DATE RANGE: 1754–1756

RARITY: Very rare

BORDER NOS: 87 and 52

MARKS: Workmen's marks

SHAPES USED: A press-moulded, two-handled, double-ended sauceboat, 7½ in. long.

COMMENTARY: While the shape of this piece is identical in every respect to the more usually decorated 'The Two-Handled Sauceboat Landscape' examples (Pattern I.B.32), the interior decoration is unique, and the exterior cartouches are also different. The only known example is that illustrated, purchased at the Sotheby sale of 20 November 1979 (Lot 127).

Sauceboat
Exterior patterns

DATE RANGE: *c.* 1765

RARITY: Uncommon

BORDER NOS: 99

MARKS: Open crescent, if any.

SHAPES USED: Press-moulded, helmet-shaped sauceboats with basket-weave exterior moulding, usually 8 in. or 8½ in. in length, as well as a smaller sauceboat, 6½ in., with different exterior moulding.

COMMENTARY: The only significant variation in the examples of this pattern which we have seen occurs in one rare version which shows an additional figure accompanying the central figure of the primary design, both painted within a slightly larger panel. This is the only pattern in underglaze blue which has been noted as occurring on this particular shape of sauceboat, which is usually very finely and thinly moulded, leading some authorities to believe that it was slip-cast. Biscuit fragments of the pattern were found in the excavations, one of which is illustrated by Sandon (Plate 90). Hobson also illustrates the pattern (Plate XXI, top left).

Sauceboat, 8¼ in. long
(Authors' Collections)

Sauceboat
Reverse pattern

Sauceboat
Interior pattern

The Willow Bridge Fisherman

DATE RANGE: 1760–1775

RARITY: Uncommon

BORDER NOS: 90

MARKS: Open crescent, or, on some later pieces, script 'W'.

SHAPES USED: Plain thrown and turned and press-moulded pieces, all of large size, including bottles of 9 in. and $10\frac{3}{4}$ in. height, gugglets (bottles with flared rims) of 11 in. height, and water ewers or jugs, $8\frac{3}{4}$ in. high. A waster was also found in the excavations of a press-moulded octagonal bottle decorated with the pattern, but no finished examples are known.

COMMENTARY: There are noticeable variations in the design and treatment of this pattern from piece to piece, expectable perhaps in a pattern that was used over such a comparatively long period. Although not illustrated here, one can see a striking example of this by comparing the two pieces sold as Lots 145 and 147 of Sotheby's sale of 28 April 1970. Biscuit and glost fragments of these pieces of all shapes were found in the excavations, sufficient in one case to reconstruct an almost complete bottle, which Sandon illustrates (Plate 17); he also illustrates the water ewer (Plate 21).

Bottle, $10\frac{3}{4}$ in. high
(Dyson Perrins Museum)

Bottle
Reverse pattern

DATE RANGE: 1754–1758

RARITY: Rare

BORDER NOS: 22 or 63 on teapots, 104 on creamboats

MARKS: Workmen's marks

SHAPES USED: The pattern is most often found on press-moulded octagonal teapots and covers, usually around 5 in. in height, but was also used to decorate a hexagonal creamboat, also press-moulded, of $4\frac{1}{2}$ in. length.

COMMENTARY: Considering the disparate shapes and sizes upon which this pattern appears, remarkably little variation in treatment or arrangement occurs, although on the smaller pieces some of the background detail is expectably omitted. Examples of both the teapot and the creamboat can be seen at the Dyson Perrins Museum. Watney illustrates a teapot and cover (Plate 23B), and also the creamboat (Plate 32B, right). Another teapot was illustrated in the catalogue of the 1979 Albert Amor Exhibition, Number 17.

Teapot and Cover, $4\frac{3}{4}$ in. high (Dyson Perrins Museum)

Creamboat
Reverse pattern

DATE RANGE: 1775–1776

RARITY: Rare

BORDER NOS: None

MARKS: Open crescent

SHAPES USED: Plain thrown and turned cylinder mugs, usually around 4½ in. high.

COMMENTARY: All known pieces decorated with this pattern have been dated – the Dyson Perrins Museum example bears the date '1776' under its handle, and other pieces, including the

Mug, 4½ in. high
(Dyson Perrins Museum)

mug in the Willett Collection at the Brighton Art Gallery and Museum in Sussex, are marked 'Ann. Dunn., Bir^m' followed by a date, either 1775 or 1776, painted along the foot of the mug. They are further decorated with stylized flower sprigs related to 'The Gilliflower/The Narcissus' subsidiary sprays (Pattern I.E.12), which are frequently employed on these documentary pieces. Hobson illustrates the Dyson Perrins example (Plate XIX, bottom right). Another example, heavily repaired, was sold by Christie's in its 12 February 1979 sale (Lot 66).

Mug
Complete pattern

I. The Painted Patterns

B. Other Figures

The Union Jack House

DATE RANGE: *c.* 1753

RARITY: Very rare

BORDER NOS: 1 at rim, 2 at base

MARKS: 'TB 1753' on base of cup.

SHAPES USED: A plain thrown and turned coffee cup, with either a plain or an elaborately modelled handle, usually around $2\frac{3}{4}$ in. high.

COMMENTARY: This early cup is decorated in a painting style very much like examples of the Lund's Bristol ware, and possibly was painted by a craftsman who joined the Worcester manufactory following the close of the Bristol concern. The only example known in a public collection is the cup illustrated. Dr Watney illustrates a plain-handled cup from his own collection (Plate 26B [right]) of his book.

Coffee Cup, $2\frac{3}{4}$ in. high
(British Museum)

Coffee Cup
Complete pattern

The High Island

Saucer, $4\frac{5}{8}$ in. diameter
(Dyson Perrins Museum)

Mustard Pot
Complete pattern

DATE RANGE: 1751–1754

RARITY: Very rare

BORDER NOS: 63 on saucer, 67 on mustard pot

MARKS: Workmen's marks

SHAPES USED: The pattern is known to occur on two plain thrown and turned shapes, the $4\frac{5}{8}$ in. diameter saucer illustrated, and a bell-shaped mustard pot, lacking cover, $3\frac{7}{8}$ in. high, with a plain handle.

COMMENTARY: It is readily apparent from a comparison of the photograph of the saucer and the tone drawing of the mustard pot that there was a considerable variation in the painting styles employed on the two pieces. However, taking account of the disparate shapes of the two, there is a remarkable consistency of arrangement and treatment in the design. The mustard pot illustrated is owned by the Victoria and Albert Museum.

The Question Mark Island

DATE RANGE: 1754–1756

RARITY: Rare

BORDER NOS: None

MARKS: Workmen's marks

SHAPES USED: Plain thrown and turned pieces, including coffee cans, teabowls and saucers, jugs, and a range of mugs from 3 in. to 6 in. in height.

COMMENTARY: Most of the examples bearing this design will be found to have been overpainted onglaze with a red or red and blue enamel. Evidence found in the excavations indicates that this overpainting was done contemporaneously with the manufacture of the pieces rather than being done at a later time, and thus does not fall within the usual definition of 'clobbering'. As far as we know, this is the only pattern where original overpainting was done as a matter of course. Both biscuit and glost wasters of the unembellished underglaze blue pattern were found, as was an example which had been overpainted. Several overpainted specimens can be seen at the Dyson Perrins Museum. Plymouth used an identical design, also overpainted in red.

Coffee Can, 2½ in. high (Private Collection)

Coffee Can Complete pattern

The Crescent Moon

Mug
Complete pattern

DATE RANGE: 1751–1754

RARITY: Rare

BORDER NOS: None

MARKS: Workmen's marks, if any.

SHAPES USED: Both thrown and turned and press-moulded shapes, including the normal range of teawares, bottles, sauceboats, mugs, and the large punch pot illustrated.

COMMENTARY: There can be a considerable disparity in this pattern as painted by different hands. You may find the primary pattern on both sides of a piece or on one side only, the reverse either being decorated with a 'bridge' design or, in the case of the punch pot illustrated, another primary pattern (here, the 'Man with a Lunchbox', Pattern I.A.24). Both biscuit and glost

fragments of the pattern were found in the factory site excavations. Watney illustrates a bottle (Plate 27B) and a teapot and cover (Plate 29C) of this design in his book.

Punch Pot, 8 in. high
(Castle Museum, Norwich)

The Full Moon

DATE RANGE: 1775–1780

RARITY: Not uncommon

BORDER NOS: 35 inside rim, 39 and 16 on exterior

MARKS: Open crescent, if any.

SHAPES USED: Press-moulded, shallow, fluted sauceboats, around 8 in. long, and elaborately decorated on the exterior.

COMMENTARY: Although of a much earlier date than this design, the influence of 'The Crescent Moon' (Pattern I.B.4) can clearly be seen here as well. Biscuit fragments of the pattern were found in the excavations of the original factory site but, despite its comparative non-rarity, we are not aware of examples within a public collection. A very similar design was done by the Derby factory, using much the same shape, so some caution is required in assuming a Worcester origin for a particular piece.

Sauceboat, 7¾ in. long
(Gilbert Bradley Collection)

Sauceboat
Exterior pattern

Sauceboat, 7 in. long
(Steppes Hill Farm Antiques)

Sauceboat
Reverse pattern

DATE RANGE: *c.* 1765

RARITY: Rare

BORDER NOS: 33

MARKS: Open crescent

SHAPES USED: Press-moulded, fluted and low-footed sauceboats, 6 in. to 7 in. in length.

COMMENTARY: Accepted by most authorities as having a Worcester origin despite the absence of confirmation from the excavations, the pattern has been illustrated by both Godden (Plate 293, bottom) and Spero (page 126). You will find a fair degree of variation between the treatment of the pattern when used on the smaller boat than that seen in the larger size illustrated here, but the design should be readily recognizable on both.

The Gazebo

DATE RANGE: 1755–1760

RARITY: Uncommon

BORDER NOS: Usually none

MARKS: Workmen's marks

SHAPES USED: A fairly wide range of teawares, all plain thrown and turned shapes.

COMMENTARY: We have provided two tone drawings of the pattern as used on different shapes to indicate the degree of variation that can be found in the treatment of the design. The standard of painting, too, can vary considerably, although on the whole the arrangement of the pattern remains fairly consistent from one piece to another. Both biscuit and glost wasters of the pattern were found in the excavations of the original factory site, and completed examples can be seen in most major public collections of porcelain including both the Dyson Perrins and Victoria and Albert Museums. Watney illustrates an interesting jug with a peaked handle (Plate 34B).

Bowl,
6 in. diameter
(Authors' Collections)

Saucer
Full pattern

Teabowl
Full pattern

The Romantic Rocks

DATE RANGE: *c.* 1755

RARITY: Rare

BORDER NOS: 72

MARKS: Workmen's marks

SHAPES USED: Octagonal press-moulded teabowls and saucers, the latter usually 4½ in. or 4¾ in. in diameter.

COMMENTARY: The design was taken from a drawing entitled 'Romantic Rocks' by Jean Pillement, an Anglo-French painter of the day, appearing in *The Ladies' Amusement*. This was a popular book of the mid-eighteenth century which contained engraved prints which could be removed and used to decorate japanned plates and trays. The Bow factory used a much more elaborate version of the same design as an onglaze transfer-print. A teabowl and saucer of the pattern were illustrated in the catalogue of the Albert Amor Blue and White Exhibition in 1979, Number 35.

*Saucer, 4½ in. diameter
(Dyson Perrins Museum)*

*Teabowl
Complete pattern*

The Rearing Rock Island

DATE RANGE: *c.* 1760

RARITY: Rare

BORDER NOS: 24

MARKS: Workmen's marks, if any.

SHAPES USED: Press-moulded, convex-fluted, low-footed sauceboats, usually $8\frac{1}{2}$ in. to $8\frac{3}{4}$ in. in length.

COMMENTARY: The arrangement of the principal details of the pieces decorated with this pattern appears to have remained consistent in the examples we have seen, although there are discernible differences in the treatment of the subject matter by the several hands that decorated these sauceboats. There is an example of the design in the collection of the Victoria and Albert Museum, and Godden illustrates another (Plate 526) in his book *British Porcelain* (see Bibliography).

Sauceboat, $8\frac{3}{4}$ in. long
(Private Collection)

Sauceboat
Reverse pattern

The Fringed Tree

Sauceboat, 7⅛ in. long
(Authors' Collections)

Sauceboat
Reverse pattern

Sauceboat
Interior pattern

DATE RANGE: 1755–1760

RARITY: Uncommon

BORDER NOS: 93

MARKS: Workmen's marks

SHAPES USED: Press-moulded, convex-fluted, low-footed sauceboats, ranging in size from 7⅛ in. to 9¾ in. in length.

COMMENTARY: Again we find that the arrangement of the principal details of the design will remain constant, although the painters who have decorated these sauceboats will tend to portray the subject matter with discernibly different styles of treatment. Examples of the pattern can be seen on sauceboats owned by the Dyson Perrins and Victoria and Albert Museums.

The Diagonal Rock Island

DATE RANGE: 1758–1760

RARITY: Very rare

BORDER NOS: 27

MARKS: Workmen's marks

SHAPES USED: Plain thrown and turned shapes, including a chocolate pot (or small coffee pot) and cover, $7\frac{1}{2}$ in. high, as illustrated, and a bowl, $4\frac{1}{8}$ in. diameter.

COMMENTARY: Although we have only seen two pieces decorated with this pattern, the chocolate pot and cover illustrated and a bowl sold by Sotheby's on 28 April 1970 as a part of the Jenkins Collection, it is reasonable to believe that the design was probably used on a complete range of tewares, including coffee cups or cans, teapots, teabowls, and the like. The chocolate pot and cover was included in the 1979 Exhibition of Blue and White Porcelain by Albert Amor Ltd, and is illustrated in the exhibition catalogue as Number 36.

Chocolate Pot and Cover, $7\frac{1}{2}$ in. high (Albert Amor Ltd)

The Treehouse

Creamboat, 4½ in. long
(Albert Amor Ltd)

Creamboat
Reverse pattern

DATE RANGE: *c.* 1760

RARITY: Very rare

BORDER NOS: 78

MARKS: Workmen's marks

SHAPES USED: A press-moulded, fluted creamboat, about 4½ in. long.

COMMENTARY: We are aware of two examples of this pattern, both on identical shapes. The creamboat illustrated was owned by Albert Amor Ltd, the London porcelain dealers, and another is in the Godden Reference Collection in Worthing. There are remarkable similarities between this design and that found on 'The Bare Tree Pagoda', reverse pattern (I.D.4). The interior of the creamboat is decorated with a small pagoda and 'club rock', also reminiscent of the later pattern.

DATE RANGE: *c.* 1755

RARITY: Rare

BORDER NOS: 92

MARKS: Workmen's marks

SHAPES USED: Press-moulded, wavy-edged, high-footed sauceboats, 8½ in. to 8¾ in. long.

COMMENTARY: Although accepted as a well-known Worcester design, examples of the pattern are rarely seen. The sauceboat illustrated was sold by Christie's in its 23 January 1978 sale (Lot 301), and another was included in the 1979 Albert Amor Ltd Exhibition as Catalogue Number 12. The Victoria and Albert Museum owns three examples of the pattern which can be seen in their collection.

Sauceboat, 8¾ in. long
(Christie, Manson and Woods Ltd)

Sauceboat
Reverse pattern

Sauceboat
Interior pattern

The Little Fisherman

DATE RANGE: *c.* 1765

RARITY: Rare

BORDER NOS: 88 inside lip, 126 on exterior

MARKS: Open crescent

SHAPES USED: Small press-moulded sauceboats, fluted and modelled, around $5\frac{1}{4}$ in. long.

COMMENTARY: You will note that the reverse design here is essentially the same as 'The Fisherman and Billboard Island' (Pattern I.B.15), reduced to fit the smaller panel. A biscuit fragment decorated with the design was found in the factory site excavation, and several complete examples are known in private collections. The sauceboat illustrated was purchased by the authors in Phillips's sale of 24 September 1978, Lot 142.

Sauceboat, $5\frac{1}{4}$ in. long (Authors' Collections)

Sauceboat
Reverse pattern

The Fisherman and Billboard Island

DATE RANGE : *c.* 1760

RARITY : Uncommon

BORDER NOS : 88 inside lip, 126 outside

MARKS : Workmen's marks, if any

SHAPES USED : Press-moulded sauceboats with strap-moulded sides and foliage-moulded cartouches, $7\frac{3}{4}$ in. to 8 in. long.

COMMENTARY : This design is essentially only an expanded version of that of the previous pattern, 'The Little Fisherman' (Pattern I.B.14), developed to fit the larger panel available. The pattern used inside the pouring spout of the sauceboat is a well-known Worcester design believed not to have been used by any other English competitor. The sauceboat illustrated in the top photograph was sold by Christie's in its 23 January 1978 sale as Lot 304. An example can be seen at the Victoria and Albert Museum.

Sauceboat, 8 in. long
(Christie, Manson and Woods Ltd)

Sauceboat, $7\frac{3}{4}$ in. long
Reverse pattern
(Private Collection)

The Prunus Tree Fisherman

Sauceboat, 5⅞ in. long
(Private Collection)

Sauceboat
Reverse pattern

DATE RANGE: 1753–1754

RARITY: Rare

BORDER NOS: 105

MARKS: Workmen's marks

SHAPES USED: Press-moulded sauceboats, usually around 6 in. long.

COMMENTARY: This early pattern is unusual in that it utilizes a prunus spray in conjunction with a figure landscape of this type, and appears to be unique from this viewpoint. There are several of these sauceboats in private collections, and there is an example in the Victoria and Albert Museum.

The Leaning Rock Fisherman

DATE RANGE: 1758–1760

RARITY: Rare

BORDER NOS: None

MARKS: Workmen's marks

SHAPES USED: A press-moulded oval potted meat pot or tub with modelled exterior, $5\frac{1}{8}$ in. long.

COMMENTARY: This pattern can also be found on tubs of a similar shape to that illustrated with entirely different exterior moulding, but the arrangement of the design will remain consistent in almost every example.

*Potted Meat Pot, $5\frac{1}{8}$ in. long
(Gilbert Bradley Collection)*

*Potted Meat Pot
Reverse pattern*

*Sauceboat, 8 in. long
(Dyson Perrins Museum)*

DATE RANGE: 1753–1755

RARITY: Very rare

BORDER NOS: 103

MARKS: None

SHAPES USED: A high-footed, wavy-edged, press-moulded sauceboat, 8 in. long.

COMMENTARY: The only example of this pattern known is on the sauceboat illustrated. It is the only sauceboat pattern of which we are aware to utilize the variety of Chinese symbols found both on the exterior and interior designs.

*Sauceboat
Reverse pattern*

*Sauceboat
Interior pattern*

The Triangular Platform

DATE RANGE: *c.* 1755

RARITY: Uncommon

BORDER NOS: 100

MARKS: Workmen's marks, if any.

SHAPES USED: Press-moulded, wavy-edged and high-footed sauceboats, $7\frac{1}{4}$ in. to $7\frac{3}{4}$ in. in length.

COMMENTARY: You will find an enormous variation in both the treatment and arrangement of this pattern on different examples, often to such a degree that recognition of the pattern can be hindered. Sandon illustrates the reverse pattern of the sauceboat (Plate 23) and Watney pictures a sauceboat with the design (Plate 28A), the latter a good example of the variation which can be experienced. Other pieces can be seen at the Dyson Perrins Museum as well as in the collection of the Victoria and Albert Museum in London.

Sauceboat, $7\frac{3}{4}$ in. long
(Authors' Collections)

Sauceboat
Reverse pattern

Sauceboat
Interior pattern

The Sinking Boat Fisherman

Sauceboat, 6¼ in. long
(Authors' Collections)

Sauceboat
Reverse pattern

Sauceboat
Interior pattern

DATE RANGE: *c.* 1755

RARITY: Uncommon

BORDER NOS: 98

MARKS: Workmen's marks

SHAPES USED: Press-moulded, wavy-edged sauceboats, both high-footed and low-footed, ranging in length from 6 in. to 8¾ in.; more rarely, the pattern is found on a press-moulded hexagonal creamboat, about 4½ in. long.

COMMENTARY: While all of the known examples employ a landscape background as an integral part of the design, these can show considerable variation in painting arrangement and treatment, and are not consistent in detail. Compare the sauceboat shown here, for example, with those illustrated by Watney (Plate 33A) and Spero (page 124) for a better understanding of the differences that can exist. Examples can be found in the Victoria and Albert Museum and the Godden Reference Collection.

The Fisherman and Willow Pavilion

DATE RANGE: 1755–1760

RARITY: Uncommon

BORDER NOS: 118

MARKS: Workmen's marks

SHAPES USED: Press-moulded, strap-fluted, teaware shapes of the usual range.

COMMENTARY: There are three landscapes that comprise this pattern, as illustrated by the photograph and two tone drawings. Bowls and saucers are usually decorated with all of these, while hollow-ware pieces such as teapots and cream jugs will only have two of them. There can be a considerable disparity in both the treatment and the arrangement of the designs, particularly noticeable in the shape and location of the pagodas that feature in two of the three landscapes. Biscuit fragments were found in the factory site excavations, and completed examples can be seen at a number of public collections of porcelain.

*Teapot and Cover, 6 in. high
(Dyson Perrins Museum)*

*Bowl
Reverse pattern, including
subsidiary birds*

*Bowl
Interior pattern*

The Indian Fisherman

Teapot and Cover, 5¼ in. high
(Dyson Perrins Museum)

Teapot and Cover
Reverse pattern

DATE RANGE: 1755–1760

RARITY: Uncommon

BORDER NOS: 109

MARKS: Workmen's marks

SHAPES USED: Press-moulded, strap-fluted teapots, ranging in size from 4¾ in. to 5¼ in. high, and cream jugs, usually 4 in. high.

COMMENTARY: Biscuit fragments of a teapot decorated with this design were found in the factory site excavations. Examples of both shapes upon which the pattern is found can be seen at the Dyson Perrins Museum, and other specimens are in the collection of the Victoria and Albert Museum. Watney illustrates the pattern (Plate 32A), and it is also shown in the catalogue of the 1979 Blue and White Exhibition of Albert Amor Ltd, Number 16.

DATE RANGE: *c.* 1760

RARITY: Very rare

BORDER NOS: 54

MARKS: Workmen's marks

SHAPES USED: A press-moulded, basket-weave junket dish with lobed edges, 9 in. diameter.

COMMENTARY: The only known example of this pattern is on the junket dish illustrated. The shape of the dish and the moulding employed are both well known at Worcester, however, and there is little doubt as to its origin.

Junket Dish, 9 in. diameter
(Gilbert Bradley Collection)

The Picture Scroll Landscape

DATE RANGE: 1755–1760

RARITY: Rare

BORDER NOS: None

MARKS: Workmen's marks

SHAPES USED: A press-moulded leaf dish, 7 in. long.

COMMENTARY: This pattern, we feel, has been adapted from that of 'The Chinese Scroll Peony' (Pattern I.D.13) to fit this particular shape of leaf dish, which has a central scroll shape moulded in relief. While there are polychrome decorated patterns utilized on this particular shape also, this is the only underglaze blue pattern used on the relief-scroll leaf dishes of this kind. Examples can be found in the Victoria and Albert Museum as well as in the Dyson Perrins Museum collection in Worcester.

Leaf Dish, 7 in. long
(Dyson Perrins Museum)

Gugglet, 11 in. high
(Godden Reference Collection)

Gugglet
Secondary pattern

Gugglet
Tertiary pattern

DATE RANGE: *c.* 1760

RARITY: Very rare

BORDER NOS: None

MARKS: Open crescent with fretted square, as illustrated.

SHAPES USED: A plain thrown and turned gugglet, 11 in. high.

COMMENTARY: The powder-blue ground technique, which was originated by the Chinese, was first used at Bow around 1760 (see Watney, Plate 12A), and it is possible that the Worcester technique was derived from that precedent. The powder-blue ground was first applied by the 'ground layer', who painted on the fretted square mark, and the crescent was added by the painter when he filled in the reserves. This is a remarkably good example of the very fine landscape painting being done by the Worcester craftsmen at this time.

Mark

The Fisherman in a Fan-Shaped Panel

DATE RANGE: 1760–1770

RARITY: Not uncommon

BORDER NOS: None

MARKS: A fretted square with an open crescent. (See Pattern I.B.25 for illustration.)

SHAPES USED: A wide range of plain, thrown and turned shapes, primarily tewares.

COMMENTARY: Examples of this well-known Worcester design can be found in several of the major public collections of English porcelains, including the Victoria and Albert Museum. Glost fragments decorated with the pattern were found in the factory site excavations, but no biscuit wasters were located. A number of authorities have illustrated the design, including Watney (Plate 36A), Sandon (Plate 98), Barrett (Plate 45), and Hobson (Plate XL, bottom left, and Plate XXXVI). See the commentary on the previous pattern (Pattern I.B.25) for remarks concerning the powder-blue ground technique.

Teapot and Cover, $5\frac{1}{2}$ in. high (Dyson Perrins Museum)

Reverse pattern

Subsidiary motifs

The Fan-Panelled Landscape

DATE RANGE: 1775–1780

RARITY: Rare

BORDER NOS: None

MARKS: A 'feathered' script 'W', as illustrated.

SHAPES USED: A press-moulded, lobed-edge plate, 9 in. diameter.

COMMENTARY: This pattern, also done in fan panels within a powder-blue ground, is more unusual than 'The Fisherman in a Fan-Panelled Landscape' (Pattern I.B.26), but possibly less unusual than 'The Arabesque Panel Landscapes' (Pattern I.B.25), both of which are found on powder-blue grounds. Godden illustrates a remarkably similar standard Bow design of the 1755–60 period (*British Porcelain*, Plate 49 [right]) which, more likely than not, was the 'inspiration' for the later Worcester pattern. A very similar design was done by the Caughley factory around 1775–80, and can only be readily distinguished by the presence of the Caughley 'C' mark which was used in addition to the same 'feathered' script 'W', clearly an effort to pass off its product as of a Worcester origin. For many years this pattern was believed to be only of Bow or Lowestoft manufacture (illustrated by Watney, Plate 77A), but has now been accepted as a Worcester design.

Plate, 9 in. diameter
(Dyson Perrins Museum)

Mark

The Cormorant

DATE RANGE: 1755–1760

RARITY: Not uncommon

BORDER NOS: None

MARKS: Workmen's marks

SHAPES USED: Plain thrown and turned shapes, primarily tewares, but including other shapes such as plates, finger-bowls and stands, cylinder and bell-shaped mugs, butter dishes, etc.

COMMENTARY: Although the pattern may appear differently when seen on a hollow-ware shape than it does when used on a piece of flatware, a closer examination will usually prove that there is little distinction in the arrangement of the overall detail, although, as an examination of the two finger-bowl stands illustrated will show, there can be remarkable differences in the treatment by individual painters. As a rule, the primary pattern will appear as the sole design on the piece, but, very rarely, there will

Finger-Bowl Stands, 5⅞ in. diameter (Christie, Manson and Woods Ltd)

be a reverse decoration as well, as illustrated on the bowl. Glost wasters decorated with the primary pattern were found in the factory site excavations, but no biscuit fragments were uncovered.

Bowl, 5½ in. diameter
Reverse pattern
(Private Collection)

Mug
Complete pattern

Bowl, 6 in. diameter
(Private Collection)

Bowl
Secondary view

Bowl
Tertiary view

DATE RANGE: *c.* 1754

RARITY: Very rare, probably unique.

BORDER NOS: None

MARKS: None

SHAPES USED: A plain thrown and turned bowl, 6 in. diameter.

COMMENTARY: This bowl, formerly in the collection of Francis and Cecele Burrell, is now owned by a private collector in London. It is painted in the European style, depicting a continuous harbour scene on two sides, with an autumnal tree on the third. As discussed in chapter 1, the style is akin to that associated with the Bristol Delft painters. There is really no comparable pattern known in this style, and it is probable that it is a unique piece rather than a pattern in the accepted sense. However, because of its importance we felt it should be included here. The bowl was illustrated in Dr Watney's book (Plate 33C), and in the Albert Amor 1979 Exhibition Catalogue as Number 6, as well as being featured in the 1977 Catalogue of the English Ceramic Circle, Plate 165.

DATE RANGE: *c.* 1765

RARITY: Rare

BORDER NOS: 25 inside lip

MARKS: Open crescent.

SHAPES USED: Press-moulded, gadroon-edged creamboats or small sauceboats, either $5\frac{1}{4}$ in. or $6\frac{1}{4}$ in. long.

COMMENTARY: A biscuit fragment having details of the pattern was uncovered in one of the early factory site excavations, but this was only matched with a complete piece when the sauceboat illustrated was offered for sale by Christie's on 19 February 1979 (Lot 34), and was purchased for the authors' collections. Since that time, one further example has been found in another private collection.

*Sauceboat, $5\frac{1}{4}$ in. long
(Authors' Collections)*

*Sauceboat
Reverse pattern*

The Two-Porter Landscape

DATE RANGE: 1760–1780

RARITY: Not uncommon

BORDER NOS: 96

MARKS: Workmen's marks on early examples, open crescents thereafter

SHAPES USED: Press-moulded creamboats, or small sauceboats, $5\frac{1}{2}$ in. long.

COMMENTARY: The quality of the painting of this pattern varies over the two decades of its use from the most careful two-tone example to the highly sketchy and rough-shod work, with miserable figures, which can be found on the later pieces. In these, the two figures are sometimes depicted in reverse, as shown in the second tone drawing. Biscuit fragments of an almost complete piece decorated with the pattern were found in the factory site excavations. Lowestoft also used the design on an identical shape, but the detail of the painting of these tended to be much poorer than even the most sketchy of the Worcester paintings.

Sauceboat, $5\frac{1}{2}$ in. long (Authors' Collections)

Sauceboat Reverse pattern

Sauceboat Variation I

Sauceboat Variation II

The Two-Handled Sauceboat Landscape

Sauceboat, 7⅓ in. long
(Phillips)

Sauceboat
Four exterior cartouche patterns

DATE RANGE: 1760–1780

RARITY: Not uncommon

BORDER NOS: 86 inside lip, 60 on exterior.

MARKS: Workmen's marks

SHAPES USED: Press-moulded, two handled, double-ended sauceboats, fluted and embossed, in a variety of sizes generally from 7¼ in. to 7¾ in. in length.

COMMENTARY: The primary variation to be found in these sauceboats, other than their size, will be in the designs of the four exterior panels, where there can be substantial differences from example to example. Except for the usual variation in painting style, the primary interior design tends to have a surprisingly consistent arrangement of detail. An undecorated biscuit waster of the shape of this two-handled sauceboat was found in the excavations, but no fragment actually decorated with the design was uncovered. The pattern has been fairly widely illustrated in various works, including those of Watney (Plate 30B) and Sandon (Plate 123), who also illustrates a polychrome example of identical shape (Plate 32).

The Six-Piered Bridge

*Basket-Bowl, 12 in. long
(Dyson Perrins Museum)*

DATE RANGE: *c.* 1755

RARITY: Very rare

BORDER NOS: 108

MARKS: None

SHAPES USED: A press-moulded, oval, basket-shaped bowl, 12 in. long, with modelled braided handles at either end.

COMMENTARY: This unusual piece is owned by a private collector but is on long-term loan to the Dyson Perrins Museum at Worcester. No other examples are known to exist which have been decorated with this particular pattern, although the basket-bowls can be found in polychrome decorated examples.

Gugglet, 9 in. high
(Private Collection)
Right: *Basin, 10¾ in. diameter*
(Sotheby Parke Bernet and Co.)

DATE RANGE: *c.* 1760

RARITY: Very rare

BORDER NOS: 81

MARKS: Workmen's marks

SHAPES USED: A plain thrown and turned wash set, including a basin, 10¾ in. diameter, and a water bottle, usually around 9 in. high.

COMMENTARY: These large basin and bottle sets are well known at Worcester, although they are more often found with a less rare pattern than that illustrated here. When sets are offered for sale, it is quite usual to find the bottle decorated with a different pattern from that on the basin, but, of course, they were made originally as a matching set with the same pattern on each.

The Dyson Perrins Museum has a basin decorated with another design which is on the identical shape to that illustrated. The basin illustrated was sold by Sotheby's on 28 April 1970 (Lot 145) in company with a bottle decorated with 'The Willow Bridge Fisherman' Pattern I.A.32).

The Cannonball Fisherman

DATE RANGE: *c.* 1773

RARITY: Very rare

BORDER NOS: None

MARKS: None

SHAPES USED: A plain thrown and turned cylinder mug, $4\frac{1}{2}$ in. high.

COMMENTARY: The only known example of this pattern is on the mug shown here and illustrated by Hobson (Plate XXI, bottom right). The pattern is a more elaborate version of the well-known 'Cannonball' (Pattern I.D.6), to which has been added the figure of a fisherman, a bridge, and an island. This piece has been inscribed and dated

T·A.

.1773.

on its base.

Mug, $4\frac{1}{2}$ in. high
(Dyson Perrins Museum)

Mug
Complete pattern

The Angler

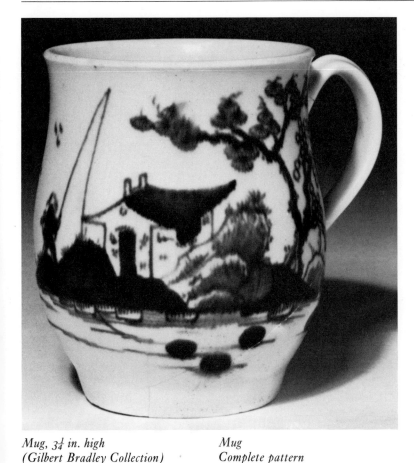

DATE RANGE: *c.* 1765

RARITY: Very rare

BORDER NOS: None

MARKS: None

SHAPES USED: A plain thrown and turned, bell-shaped mug, $3\frac{1}{4}$ in. high.

COMMENTARY: The three blue 'boulders' in the foreground of the design are similar to those found in 'The Cannonball' (Pattern I.D.6) and its closely linked 'The Cannonball Fisherman' (Pattern I.B.35) preceding. However, that appears to be the only connection between these, as the treatment and arrangement of the two designs are otherwise quite different.

Mug, $3\frac{1}{4}$ in. high
(Gilbert Bradley Collection)

Mug
Complete pattern

The Club Rock Patty Pan

DATE RANGE: *c.* 1765

RARITY: Very rare

BORDER NOS: 85

MARKS: None

SHAPES USED: A plain thrown and turned patty pan, about 4 in. diameter.

COMMENTARY: The only example of this pattern which we have seen is on the patty pan illustrated, which was owned some years ago by Simon Spero of China Choice Antiques in London. The shape of the pan is identical to those decorated with the more common patterns, and the similarity of the details of the design to others illustrated here leaves little doubt as to its Worcester origin.

*Patty Pan, 4 in. diameter
(China Choice Antiques)*

The Bare Tree and Speared Bird

Patty Pan, 4 in. diameter
(Dyson Perrins Museum)

DATE RANGE: 1758–1765

RARITY: Uncommon

BORDER NOS: 29

MARKS: Workmen's marks on the earliest examples, open crescents thereafter.

SHAPES USED: A plain thrown and turned patty pan of 4 in. diameter, or, more rarely, a larger patty pan of $4\frac{5}{8}$ in. diameter.

COMMENTARY: The pattern, which is remarkably consistent on known examples, was apparently used only on this patty pan shape, and, further, is the only other pattern of which we are aware to utilize the border employed on the 'Mansfield' floral design (Pattern I.E.1). The 'speared bird' motif can be found on at least two other Worcester designs, 'The Walk in the Garden' (Pattern I.A.17) and the reverse pattern of 'The Willow Bridge Fisherman' (Pattern I.A.32). Glost wasters, but no biscuit fragments, were found in the factory site excavations, and complete examples can be seen at the Victoria and Albert Museum among others.

The Caughley Temple

DATE RANGE: 1780–1790

RARITY: Rare

BORDER NOS: 38

MARKS: Usually none

SHAPES USED: A variety of press-moulded, fluted shapes, including teawares such as a teapoy and cover, saucers, fluted bowls such as that illustrated, as well as a larger bowl of $6\frac{3}{4}$ in., and a milk jug. More rarely, it was used on a plain thrown and turned coffee pot, the cover of which was found in one of the factory site excavations.

COMMENTARY: This is Worcester's *painted* version of the Caughley printed 'Bridge' (or as it is now called, 'Temple') pattern, rather than a painted rendition of Worcester's own 'Temple' design (Pattern II.B.11), which is quite different. The Worcester painter(s) responsible for this decoration have gone to great lengths to duplicate the Caughley pattern's printed lines, leaving little doubt that this was a deliberate attempt to copy the work of the rival factory. The only explanation we can offer as to why Worcester decided to paint the design rather than use the expectable printing technique is that they wished to avoid the blurring of the pattern which so often occurred when a printed transfer was applied to a fluted shape. Godden illustrates the Caughley print (Plates 17 and 18). Glost fragments of the Worcester pattern were found in the factory site excavations, as noted.

Bowl, 6 in. diameter ▶
(Dyson Perrins Museum)

Bowl
Complete pattern

The Two Men on a Hump-Backed Bridge

DATE RANGE: 1785–1790

RARITY: Very rare

BORDER NOS: 53

MARKS: None

SHAPES USED: A press-moulded, octagonal plate, 8½ in. diameter.

COMMENTARY: This pattern, like that of the preceding 'Caughley Temple' (Pattern I.B.39), is distinctive in the meticulous care that has been taken in rendering the linear-style design, as if it were intended as a copied replacement of a broken or missing piece from an existing service. The Chaffers factory at Liverpool used a pattern which is very close to the Worcester design (see Watney, Plate 56C), but is somewhat less elaborate, and both may have been taken from the same source, most probably a Chinese original.

Plate, 8½ in. diameter
(Authors' Collections)

I. The Painted Patterns

C. Birds and Animals

The Swimming Ducks

DATE RANGE: 1751–1753

RARITY: Very rare

BORDER NOS: None

MARKS: Workmen's marks

SHAPES USED: The only known example decorated with this pattern is the plain thrown and turned coffee can, 2½ in. high, illustrated. However, a biscuit fragment of a teabowl of the design was found in the factory site excavations.

COMMENTARY: This pattern is an ideal illustration of the sketchy, naïve, and somewhat primitive style of painting inherited by the Worcester enterprise from its Lund's Bristol predecessor, discussed in chapter 1.

Coffee Can, 2½ in. high
(Victoria and Albert Museum)

Coffee Can
Complete pattern

DATE RANGE: 1751–1755

RARITY: Very rare

BORDER NOS: 101

MARKS: None

SHAPES USED: A press-moulded, wavy-edged, high-footed sauceboat, 8 in. long.

COMMENTARY: The only known example of this pattern is the sauceboat illustrated. A biscuit fragment of a small part of the pattern was found in the excavations of the original factory site, clearly confirming its Worcester origin.

Sauceboat, 8 in. long
(Victoria and Albert Museum)

Sauceboat
Reverse pattern

Sauceboat
Interior pattern

The Creamboat Warbler

DATE RANGE: 1753–1755

RARITY: Very rare

BORDER NOS: 107

MARKS: None

SHAPES USED: Press-moulded creamboats or small sauceboats, both in fluted form with a scroll handle, about 5 in. long, as illustrated, and of a plainer shape with an angular handle and small foot, around the same length.

COMMENTARY: The warbler-like bird, after which the pattern is named, appears on the front of the sauceboat beneath the pouring lip, as illustrated by the tone drawing. The pattern is consistently arranged on each of the two shapes which it decorates, and the use of the 'warbler' motif suggests some artistic link to the better known 'Warbler' pattern (I.C.4) hereafter. However, the remainder of the design is really rather different from that pattern, and has a much closer stylistic relationship to the 'Weeping Willow' (Pattern I.D.22).

Creamboat, 5 in. long
(Godden Reference Collection)

Creamboat
Reverse pattern

DATE RANGE: 1754–1760

RARITY: Uncommon

BORDER NOS: 63

MARKS: Workmen's marks

SHAPES USED: Plain thrown and turned shapes, usually on bowls of either $5\frac{1}{4}$ in. or $7\frac{1}{2}$ in. diameters, but more rarely on teabowls and saucers, ear-handled coffee cups, and saucer dishes.

COMMENTARY: There can be some variation in the arrangement of this pattern on different shapes, as can be seen by comparing the tone drawing of the complete pattern of the Dyson Perrins Museum's bowl with the photograph of the saucer, noting that in the latter the fence emerges from the opposite side of the rock than that on the bowl. The painting is not too skilfully done, unlike other similar designs used during the early years of the Worcester manufactory. Spero illustrates a teabowl and saucer decorated with the pattern (page 156), and Dr Watney shows the smaller size of bowl (Plate 24B).

Saucer, $4\frac{1}{2}$ in. diameter
(Gilbert Bradley Collection)

▲ *Bowl, $7\frac{1}{2}$ in. diameter*
(Dyson Perrins Museum)

▼ *Bowl*
Complete pattern

The Rock Warbler

DATE RANGE: 1754–1760

RARITY: Uncommon

BORDER NOS: Usually none

MARKS: Workmen's marks

SHAPES USED: Plain thrown and turned shapes, primarily teawares like the coffee can illustrated, large bowls, sparrowbeak jugs, and a complete set of miniature teawares.

COMMENTARY: It is entirely possible that this design is simply an amalgamation of 'The Warbler' (Pattern I.C.4) and 'The Prunus Fence' (Pattern I.D.16) as it contains elements found in each. There appears to be little variation of arrangement or treatment in the examples we have seen, all of which have been generally well painted and crisply executed. A biscuit waster of the design was found in one of the early factory site excavations. Spero illustrates a miniature teapot (page 153), and several other examples can be seen in the collections of the Dyson Perrins and Victoria and Albert Museums.

Coffee Can, 2½ in. high
(Dyson Perrins Museum)

Bowl
Complete pattern

The Zig-Zag Fence Bird

Plate, 9 in. diameter
(Albert Amor Ltd)

DATE RANGE: 1753–1755

RARITY: Very rare

BORDER NOS: 84

MARKS: A pseudo-Chinese mark, consisting of a 'precious objects' symbol and a further Chinese character within a double ring on the base.

SHAPES USED: A plain-rimmed plate, 9 in. in diameter.

COMMENTARY: This pattern is a near relation of the well-known 'Zig-Zag Fence' (Pattern I.D.12), and is distinctive primarily because of the inclusion of a warbler-type bird amidst the branches of the peony sprays. Like 'The Writhing Rock' (Pattern I.A.5), there is a strong flavour here of the style of painting used by the Dutch and the Bristol Delft painters during the earlier part of the eighteenth century. The plate illustrated was included, as Number 26, in the Albert Amor Ltd 1979 Exhibition of Blue and White Soft Paste Porcelains, and Dr Watney illustrates a further example (Plate 25C).

The Peony Rock Bird

*Tureen and Cover, 18 in. long
(Dyson Perrins Museum)*

DATE RANGE: 1755–1758

RARITY: Very rare

BORDER NOS: None

MARKS: Workmen's marks

SHAPES USED: A press-moulded
tureen and cover, 18 in. long, with
modelled handles and an unusual
gnarled branch knop.

COMMENTARY: This
exceptionally finely painted design
decorates a large moulded tureen
and cover which allows much
room for full artistic expression.
The pattern combines many
motifs of previous designs – birds,
trees, rocks, etc. – which
Worcester continued to use for
several years in its painted
patterns. The rendering of the
work, however, is sufficiently
stylized to lead us to believe that
this was not a unique example,
but rather was intended for use as
a pattern for other similar large
pieces.

Chestnut–Basket Stand, 10 in. long
Complete pattern

DATE RANGE: 1765–1770

RARITY: Very rare

BORDER NOS: 34

MARKS: Open crescent

SHAPES USED: A press-moulded, pierced, and decorated chestnut-basket stand with applied flowers, 10 in. long.

COMMENTARY: Only one complete example of this basket stand is known, illustrated by Dr Watney (Plate 37B) along with the chestnut basket which accompanied it. However, there was an almost complete stand found in the factory site excavations at Worcester, and it was from this that the tone drawing was made. A picture of the waster stand is shown by Sandon (Plate 122). As we have not been able to examine either the basket or the basket stand illustrated by Dr Watney, we do not know whether the basket's interior base in any way matched the decoration of the stand or, more expectably, was only painted with a floral spray.

The Willow Rock Bird

DATE RANGE: 1758–1765

RARITY: Uncommon

BORDER NOS: 65

MARKS: Either workmen's marks
or open crescents.

SHAPES USED: Press-moulded
hors d'oeuvres trays of slightly
differing shapes, ranging in size
from $2\frac{3}{4}$ in. to $3\frac{1}{2}$ in. in width.

COMMENTARY: These trays
were a part of a set of six,
arranged in a circular interlock
around a star-shaped centrepiece,
almost always decorated with
'The *Hors d'Oeuvres* Centre'
(Pattern I.D.24). This pattern
tended to be rather freely painted,
and, as can be seen in the tone
drawings, significant variations
occurred in different examples
adding great difficulty for any
collector who wishes to assemble a
matched complete set. One such
set, including the centrepiece
which was not entirely matching
in painting style, was featured in
the Albert Amor 1979 Blue and

White Exhibition, Catalogue
Number 63. Both biscuit and
glost wasters of the pattern were
found in the excavations, one of
which has been included in our
photograph.

*Three Hors d'Oeuvres Trays, $2\frac{3}{4}$ in.
to $3\frac{1}{2}$ in. wide
(Dyson Perrins Museum)*

*Three Hors d'Oeuvres Trays
Painting variations*

The Two-Peony Rock Bird

Shell Tray, 6¼ in. diameter
(Sotheby Parke Bernet and Co.)

DATE RANGE: 1754–1765

RARITY: Uncommon

BORDER NOS: 26

MARKS: Workmen's marks on the earlier examples, open crescents thereafter.

SHAPES USED: Press-moulded trays of two types, one shell-shaped as illustrated in a range of sizes from 3¾ in. to 6¼ in. diameter, and, more rarely, leaf-shaped trays of either 4 in. or 4¾ in. diameter.

COMMENTARY: While the arrangement of the details of this pattern remained fairly constant over the relatively long period of its manufacture, one can note significant variations in the painting treatment of the subject matter between the earlier and later examples. Several examples of the pattern can be seen at the Dyson Perrins and the Victoria and Albert Museums, and Spero illustrates a smaller sized shell tray (page 149).

The Hollow Rock Lily

DATE RANGE: 1760–1775

RARITY: Common

BORDER NOS: 74

MARKS: Usually open crescents, although some earlier pieces will be found with workmen's marks.

SHAPES USED: The pattern is only used on jolleyed and press-moulded, concave-fluted teawares of the usual range, including bowls of up to 6 in. diameter, and 5 in. and 7 in. saucer dishes.

COMMENTARY: This was a popular pattern over a comparatively long period, and, expectably, one will find a considerable variation in the treatment of the subject matter, although the arrangement of the details of the design remain fairly constant. In the later pieces the painting becomes somewhat haphazard, particularly noticeable in the rendering of the foreground of the design. Quantities of both biscuit and glost fragments were

uncovered in the factory site excavations, and Sandon illustrates one of these wasters (Plate 104), alongside a completed teabowl and saucer.

Saucer Dish, 7 in. diameter (Dyson Perrins Museum)

*Teabowl
Complete pattern*

Teabowl, 3 in. diameter
(Authors' Collections)

Teabowl
Complete pattern

DATE RANGE: 1765–1770

RARITY: Rare

BORDER NOS: 68

MARKS: Open crescent

SHAPES USED: A jolleyed, feather-moulded teabowl, and, most probably other teawares.

COMMENTARY: The feather-moulded shape decorated with this pattern was frequently used at Worcester. The pattern itself is very closely related to that of 'The Inverted Floral' (Pattern I.E.36), differing primarily through the addition of the long-tailed birds, but otherwise rendered in much the same style of painting. The example illustrated was purchased at the Phillips's sale of 13 February 1980. To our knowledge, no examples of this pattern are to be found in the major public collections of porcelain.

The Prunus Branch Bird

DATE RANGE: *c.* 1753

RARITY: Rare

BORDER NOS: None

MARKS: Workmen's marks

SHAPES USED: A fluted coffee can, probably press-moulded rather than jolleyed, 2¼ in. high.

COMMENTARY: Neither the photograph nor the tone drawing shows the bird which appears on the front of this coffee can, very similar in style to those of 'The Feather Mould Birds' (Pattern I.C.12) preceding. Otherwise, however, the pattern has a closer relationship to the decoration on 'The Cornucopia Prunus' (Pattern I.E.20). The coffee can illustrated is in the Godden Reference Collection in Worthing. An example was sold by Christie's on 23 January 1978 (Lot 270).

Coffee Can, 2¼ in. high
(Godden Reference Collection)

Coffee Can
Reverse pattern

The Bird in a Ring

*Saucer, $4\frac{4}{5}$ in. diameter
(Gilbert Bradley Collection)*

*Bowl
Complete pattern*

DATE RANGE: 1760–1770

RARITY: Not uncommon

BORDER NOS: 60

MARKS: Open crescent

SHAPES USED: Plain thrown and turned tewares of the usual range.

COMMENTARY: There is a most remarkable lack of variation in this pattern, both in its treatment and arrangement, and the discernible differences to be found from example to example are very small indeed. The uniformity was probably due to the simple linear style with which the design was rendered, similar in this respect to 'The Cannonball' (Pattern I.D.6), which also retained a remarkable uniformity over an even longer period of manufacture. To our knowledge, Worcester was the only English porcelain maker to use this design. Both biscuit and glost fragments with the decoration were found in the excavations of the original factory site.

The Two Quails

DATE RANGE: *c.* 1775

RARITY: Uncommon

BORDER NOS: 9

MARKS: Open crescent

SHAPES USED: Plain thrown and turned teawares of the usual range.

COMMENTARY: Although a number of contemporary porcelain manufacturers in England used a decoration featuring one or more quail-like birds, most of these are easily distinguishable from the Worcester design which, while somewhat dashingly painted, shows little variation in treatment or arrangement in different examples. Fragments decorated with the design were found in both the biscuit and glost state in the factory site excavations, and the pattern has been illustrated widely, including Sandon (Plate 94), Severne Mackenna (Plate 27) and Watney (Plate 35C). Examples of the pattern can be found in several of the major public collections of English porcelains.

*Saucer, 5 in. diameter
(Dyson Perrins Museum)*

The Wading Birds

DATE RANGE: *c.* 1756

RARITY: Very rare, perhaps unique

BORDER NOS: None

MARKS: None

SHAPES USED: A thrown and turned finger bowl with lobed rim, $3\frac{1}{4}$ in. diameter, 3 in. high.

COMMENTARY: Although no fragment bearing this exact design was found in the course of the several excavations of the waster pits of the original factory, a biscuit piece decorated with similar birds, quite possibly by the same painter, was uncovered there. There is a strong relationship between the style of this painting and the pattern which follows ('The Cranes Among Reeds', Pattern I.C.17), with which this should be compared. The finger bowl illustrated is the only known example of this pattern.

Finger Bowl, $3\frac{1}{4}$ in. diameter (Dyson Perrins Museum)

Finger Bowl
Complete pattern

The Cranes Among Reeds

DATE RANGE: *c.* 1756

RARITY: Very rare, perhaps unique

BORDER NOS: None

MARKS: Workmen's marks

SHAPES USED: A thrown and turned pear-shaped dry mustard pot with domed cover, $4\frac{3}{4}$ in. high.

COMMENTARY: The only known example of this pattern is on the dry mustard pot illustrated. It was lent for the 1979 Albert Amor Exhibition of Blue and White English Porcelain, and catalogued there as Number 30. It is also illustrated in Rissik Marshall, Plate 3(50). The stylistic connection between the birds painted on this pot and those on the 'Wading Birds' finger bowl (Pattern I.C.16) is quite obvious.

Mustard Pot and Cover, $4\frac{3}{4}$ in. high (Ashmolean Museum)

The Heron on a Floral Spray

Saucer, $4\frac{3}{4}$ in. diameter
(Dyson Perrins Museum)

DATE RANGE: *c.* 1758

RARITY: Very rare

BORDER NOS: 21

MARKS: Workmen's marks

SHAPES USED: The pattern is known on four shapes, all plain and thrown tearwares, including the saucer illustrated, a 3 in. diameter teabowl, a plain coffee cup $2\frac{1}{2}$ in. high, and a waste bowl, around $4\frac{7}{8}$ in. diameter.

COMMENTARY: It is probable that this pattern was derived from a Chinese original design, although we have not been able to locate its source. Bow used the pattern with a polychrome decoration, probably from the same origin as the Worcester version. The coffee cup mentioned was included in the 1979 Albert Amor Exhibition as Item 46, and the teabowl and waste bowl are both in private collections.

DATE RANGE: 1758–1760

RARITY: Uncommon

BORDER NOS: Own border related to 65

MARKS: Workmen's marks, imitation Meissen 'crossed sword' marks, and, on later pieces, open crescents.

SHAPES USED: The design was used only on large hexagonal and octagonal press-moulded shapes, including hexagonal vases and covers such as those illustrated, ranging from 15 in. to 16 in. in height, and on octagonal jardinieres between $10\frac{1}{2}$ in. and $12\frac{1}{2}$ in. high, with an accompanying stand, 14 in. diameter and $2\frac{1}{2}$ in. high.

COMMENTARY: A number of biscuit wasters decorated with this design were found in the factory excavations, one of which is illustrated by Sandon (Colour Plate 1). The pattern has also been illustrated by Severne Mackenna (Plate 23) and by Hobson (Plate XVIII, bottom). The treatment of the design shows no great variation from example to example, although it has necessarily been altered to adapt to the quite different shapes on which it was used. The knops on the vase covers illustrated have been replaced; originally they were painted blue from the top of the knop to about three-quarters of its length.

Pair, Vases and Covers, $15\frac{1}{2}$ in. high (Phillips)

Vase
Complete pattern

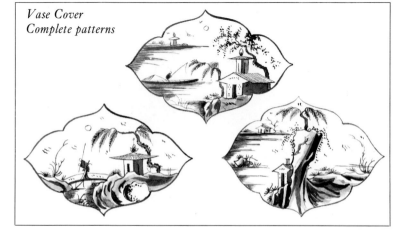

Vase Cover
Complete patterns

DATE RANGE: *c.* 1753

RARITY: Very rare

BORDER NOS: None

MARKS: None

SHAPES USED: A plain thrown and turned, bell-shaped mug, $4\frac{3}{4}$ in. high.

COMMENTARY: The only example of this pattern we have seen is on the bell-shaped mug illustrated. From the characteristics of the mug itself, and the strong relationship which the design has to the pattern following ('The Nesting Crane', Pattern I.C.21), we think there is little doubt as to its Worcester origin, despite its bright blue colouration.

Mug, $4\frac{3}{4}$ in. high
(Gilbert Bradley Collection)

Mug
Complete pattern

The Nesting Crane

DATE RANGE: *c.* 1758

RARITY: Very rare

BORDER NOS: None

MARKS: Workmen's marks

SHAPES USED: Plain thrown and turned cylinder mugs, either $4\frac{1}{2}$ in. or $4\frac{3}{4}$ in. high.

COMMENTARY: We must confess to some lingering doubts as to whether this is really a pattern separate and apart from 'The Nesting Bird' that precedes this (Pattern I.C.20), but despite the strong links between the two, we feel that there are sufficient differences to justify separating them. The only example of this pattern known in a public collection is in Trerice House, a National Trust establishment near Newquay, Cornwall. Another was sold by Sotheby's on 7 October 1969, Lot 159, and the example illustrated was in Phillips's sale of 26 March 1980, Lot 192.

Mug, $4\frac{1}{2}$ in. high
(Phillips)

Mug
Complete pattern

*Creamboat, 4 in. long
(Gilbert Bradley Collection)*

DATE RANGE: 1755–1758

RARITY: Rare

BORDER NOS: 106

MARKS: Workmen's marks, if any.

SHAPES USED: Press-moulded creamboats, 4 in. long.

COMMENTARY: The few creamboats that we have seen decorated with this design show little variety in either their treatment or arrangement. Two examples of the pattern, one of which has been 'clobbered' by the later addition of onglaze enamels, are owned by the Dyson Perrins Museum and Dr Watney illustrates another (Plate 32B [left]).

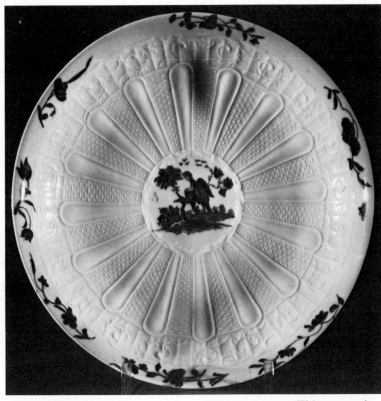

*Saucer Dish, 8 in. diameter
(Godden Reference Collection)*

DATE RANGE: *c.* 1757

RARITY: Very rare

BORDER NOS: III

MARKS: Workmen's marks

SHAPES USED: A jolleyed saucer dish, 8 in. diameter.

COMMENTARY: This pattern is found on a saucer dish with a highly unusual moulded shape, possibly based on a design used in silver-making. The decoration itself is suggestive of the style of painting seen in greater detail on such patterns as 'The Mobbing Birds' (Pattern I.C.26) and is definitely of that genre. Mr Godden has shown a very similar saucer dish as Plate 522 of his book *British Porcelain* (see Bibliography).

*Spoon Tray, 5½ in. long
(Albert Amor Ltd)*

DATE RANGE: *c.* 1757

RARITY: Very rare

BORDER NOS: None

MARKS: Unknown

SHAPES USED: A press-moulded
spoon tray, about 5½ in. long.

COMMENTARY: The spoon tray
illustrated was sold some years
ago by Albert Amor Ltd, the
London porcelain dealers, and its
present ownership is unknown to
us. The shape of the tray is
known at Worcester with
polychrome decoration, although
these pieces are also very rare.
The style of painting, which is
similar to 'The Watchful Bird'
preceding (Pattern I.C.23)
certainly suggests a Worcester
origin.

The Thrush

DATE RANGE: *c.* 1760

RARITY: Rare

BORDER NOS: None

MARKS: Workmen's marks, if any.

SHAPES USED: Plain thrown and turned teapots with a faceted spout, and cover with a flower bud finial amidst two moulded leaves, the height ranging from $5\frac{1}{4}$ in. to $5\frac{1}{2}$ in.

COMMENTARY: You will find that the primary pattern can be used interchangeably on different examples, the teapot illustrated having the birds pictured on the right side of the spout, and the example in the Dyson Perrins Museum with the birds on the reverse. Another teapot and cover was included in the Albert Amor 1979 Exhibition of English Blue and White Porcelain, Catalogue Number 62. The example illustrated was owned by Hoff Antiques Ltd, porcelain dealers in London, and sold to a private collector in 1979.

Teapot and Cover, $5\frac{1}{4}$ in. high
(Hoff Antiques Ltd)

Teapot
Reverse subject

The Mobbing Birds

DATE RANGE: 1757–1760

RARITY: Rare

BORDER NOS: None

MARKS: Workmen's marks on most pieces, possibly open crescents on later examples.

SHAPES USED: Plain thrown and turned garniture sets and other ornamental shapes, primarily spill vases, covered vases of around 8 in. height, and plain vases such as that illustrated, which may originally have been supplied with a cover as well.

COMMENTARY: The Worcester factory used a very similar design in its onglaze polychrome decorated pieces, perhaps the

Vase, 6 in. high
(Dyson Perrins Museum)

source for the blue and white version illustrated. There are two variants of the design, one as shown here, the other having an owl perched on the upper branches of the tree ('The Mobbing Birds with Owl', Pattern I.C.27). The painted version was adapted for use as an onglaze transfer-print some years later, and rarely can be found as the reverse pattern on large pieces decorated with 'The Birds in Branches' print (Pattern II.B.21). Examples can be found in the collections of the British Museum and the Victoria and Albert Museum. Watney illustrates a spill vase decorated with the pattern (Plate 31B).

Vase
Complete pattern

The Mobbing Birds with Owl

DATE RANGE: 1757–1760

RARITY: Rare

BORDER NOS: None

MARKS: Workmen's marks on most examples, possibly open crescents on later pieces.

SHAPES USED: Plain thrown and turned garniture sets and other ornamental shapes, most often on a vase and cover similar to that illustrated, about 8 in. high.

COMMENTARY: As a rule, the owl will be found to have been added to the larger covered vases in the garniture set, and missing from the smaller side vases, which will be decorated with the pattern preceding (I.C.26); however, this is not always the case, so we have shown this design separately rather than as an integral part of a garniture painting. This painting as well as that of the previous pattern is often attributed to the hand of James Rogers, a celebrated painter of bird scenes during the period. While possibly true, there were a number of craftsmen at the Worcester factory who were quite capable of the skills exhibited in the examples decorated with this design, so it would not be possible to make a definite attribution on the basis of the evidence available.

Vase with Cover, 8 in. high
(Victoria and Albert Museum)

*Tureen and Cover, 10 in. diameter
(Sotheby Parke Bernet and Co.)*

*Tureen and Cover, 10 in.
diameter
Reverse pattern
(Sotheby Parke Bernet and Co.)*

DATE RANGE: 1754–1755

RARITY: Very rare

BORDER NOS: None

MARKS: Workmen's marks

SHAPES USED: Plain thrown and turned tureens with moulded handles, 10 in. diameter, and covers with either modelled rose knops, fish, or twig-shaped finials.

COMMENTARY: The tureen and cover illustrated in the photograph above was sold by Sotheby's as a part of the Jenkins Collection on 28 April 1970 (Lot 153), and another tureen with the same decoration but having a twig-shaped finial (the photograph below) was offered for sale at Sotheby's on 8 April 1975. We know of three other examples, two of which are in private collections in England, and the other, with a fish finial on its cover, in private ownership in the United States. Here, too, the painting is frequently attributed to the hand of James Rogers, although we feel it equally likely that the decoration was actually done by one of several highly skilled craftsmen at the Worcester factory.

The Eight Horses of Mu Wang

DATE RANGE: *c.* 1775

RARITY: Very rare

BORDER NOS: 125

MARKS: The pattern has its own unique mark, as illustrated.

SHAPES USED: Press-moulded dishes of a dessert service, either heart (or 'kidney') shaped, or oval, as in the illustration. They ranged in length from 10 in. to $10\frac{1}{2}$ in.

COMMENTARY: This design is a careful Worcester copy of a K'ang

Hsi original, used earlier by the Bristol Delft painters on pottery. The William Ball factory at Liverpool also made a 'Mu Wang' design (see Watney, Plate 49B), which is quite different and easily distinguishable from that shown here. For many years this pattern was believed to have originated at the Derby factory, but is now generally accepted to have had a Worcester origin. Examples of the pattern can also be seen at the Victoria and Albert Museum, and another was illustrated in the Catalogue of the 1979 Albert Amor Exhibition of Blue and White Porcelain, Item 53.

*Oval Dish, 10 in. long
(Dyson Perrins Museum)*

Mark

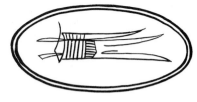

The Blue Valentine

DATE RANGE: 1760–1765

RARITY: Very rare

BORDER NOS: 34

MARKS: Open crescent

SHAPES USED: Plain thrown and turned teawares, including the saucer dish illustrated, a $2\frac{1}{2}$ in. high coffee cup, and an $8\frac{1}{2}$ in. coffee pot.

COMMENTARY: The only example of this rare pattern known in a public collection is the saucer dish illustrated; all other examples are in private collections. There is some stylistic similarity between this blue and white design and the better known Worcester onglaze polychrome 'Valentine' pattern, which was taken from a Chinese original and from which the blue and white version takes its name.

Saucer Dish, 7 in. diameter
(Dyson Perrins Museum)

Coffee Cup
Complete pattern

The Dragon

Stand, 4¼ in. diameter
(Dyson Perrins Museum)

Mug
Complete pattern

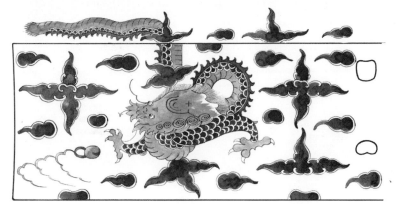

DATE RANGE: 1758–1765

RARITY: Uncommon

BORDER NOS: None

MARKS: Workmen's marks on early examples, open crescents thereafter.

SHAPES USED: A fairly wide range of plain thrown and turned shapes, including saucer dishes, cylinder mugs of various sizes, tea-bowls, saucers, and other teawares.

COMMENTARY: This was a popular design during the latter half of the eighteenth century and most English factories used the pattern. It is not possible to judge whether the Worcester pattern was derived from the early Bow design, or was taken from the Chinese original, the source of all of the English 'Dragon' patterns. However, as Bow used a crescent mark on their later examples of this pattern, there is some evidence that they may have been copying Worcester, at least at that particular time. You will note that, in some examples (see the tone drawing of the mug), the scales of the dragon are carefully and individually painted, while on others (like the stand illustrated), they have been washed in with a lighter cobalt and simply outlined with darker blue. As noted in chapter 1, Worcester experimented with painting this design in underglaze manganese, but the surviving pieces so decorated are exceedingly rare. Biscuit fragments of the underglaze blue design were found in the factory site excavations.

DATE RANGE: *c.* 1755

RARITY: Very rare

BORDER NOS: 117

MARKS: Workmen's marks

SHAPES USED: Plain thrown and turned porringers (or, perhaps, bleeding bowls), $5\frac{1}{4}$ in. diameter, with either a press-moulded and highly modelled handle or a plainer version.

COMMENTARY: This unusual design was first used in England by the Bristol Delft painters on pottery, having borrowed it from a Chinese original of some years earlier. The Victoria and Albert Museum also have an example, and Dr Watney illustrated it (Plate 25B). There was no excavation evidence to support a Worcester origin, but examples of other porringers can be found decorated with different patterns which can be supported with such evidence.

Porringer, $5\frac{1}{4}$ in. diameter
(Dyson Perrins Museum)

Porringer
Exterior pattern

I. The Painted Patterns

D. Landscapes

Bowl, 4⅛ in. diameter
(Private Collection)

Bowl
Complete pattern

DATE RANGE: 1752–1753

RARITY: Very rare

BORDER NOS: None

MARKS: None

SHAPES USED: Plain thrown and turned shapes, including the bowl illustrated, a larger bowl of 5 in. diameter, and a coffee cup.

COMMENTARY: This early pattern displays the typically primitive and simply drawn style expectable at this point of the factory's development. It has a close relationship to the paintings found on other early designs like 'The Primitive Chinaman' (Pattern I.A.1) and 'The Union Jack House' (Pattern I.B.1), but unlike these, has no figure in the arrangement.

DATE RANGE: 1755–1757

RARITY: Very rare

BORDER NOS: 95

MARKS: Workmen's marks

SHAPES USED: A press-moulded sauceboat, probably about $7\frac{3}{4}$ in. in length in its original state.

COMMENTARY: This is the only landscape scene which does not include a figure to have been used to decorate this particular shape of sauceboat, but the style of painting and the general design of the pattern is nevertheless akin to that found on 'The Fisherman on a Towering Rock' (Pattern I.B.13), 'The Triangular Platform' (Pattern I.B.19) and other patterns of that type.

Sauceboat, 7 in. long
(Private Collection)

Sauceboat
Interior pattern

Sauceboat
Reverse pattern

Butterboat, 3¼ in. long
(Godden Reference Collection)

DATE RANGE: *c.* 1758

RARITY: Very rare

BORDER NOS: 127

MARKS: Workmen's marks

SHAPES USED: A press-moulded, leaf-shaped butterboat, 3¼ in. long.

COMMENTARY: The upright rock in the foreground appears to be an afterthought by the painter, as the background island and tree trunks can be clearly seen through it as though the rock were made of glass, hence its name. The only known example of this pattern is that illustrated.

The Bare Tree Pagoda

DATE RANGE: *c.* 1760

RARITY: Uncommon

BORDER NOS: 79

MARKS: Open crescent

SHAPES USED: Press-moulded hexagonal creamboats, 4 in. to $4\frac{1}{4}$ in. long.

COMMENTARY: This is another pattern where the two designs on front and reverse are used interchangeably, as you will see if you compare the sauceboat illustrated with that shown in Spero (page 122). There are some similarities between this design and that of 'The Treehouse' (Pattern I.B.12), but they are clearly separate patterns. There are also examples of the pattern in the Dyson Perrins Museum, the Victoria and Albert Museum and in the private collection of Gilbert Bradley in London. A glost waster decorated with the design was found in the factory site excavations.

Creamboat, 4 in. long
(Godden Reference Collection)

Creamboat
Reverse pattern

The Pylon Trees

Sauceboat, 6¼ in. long
Reverse pattern
(Dyson Perrins Museum)

Sauceboat
Primary pattern

DATE RANGE: *c.* 1755

RARITY: Very rare

BORDER NOS: 91

MARKS: Workmen's marks, if any

SHAPES USED: Press-moulded, convex-fluted, low-footed sauceboats, 6¼ in. long.

COMMENTARY: A biscuit fragment showing a very small part of this pattern was found in one of the early factory site excavations. You will note from the comparison of the tone drawing with the photograph that the reverse pattern is the same, except that it is drawn in mirror image. The Bow factory made a version of the design around 1753 (see Watney, Plate 6D) which may have been the source for the Worcester pattern, believed to have been made some one or two years later.

Teapot and Cover, 5 in. high
(Dyson Perrins Museum)

Saucer
Complete pattern

DATE RANGE: 1755–1780

RARITY: Common

BORDER NOS: 60

MARKS: Workmen's marks on the earlier pieces, open crescents and script 'W' marks on the later ones.

SHAPES USED: An almost complete range of teawares, together with small cylinder mugs about 4½ in. high.

COMMENTARY: The 'Cannonball' design was widely used by the English porcelain makers during the latter half of the eighteenth century, and versions can be found from the Chaffers-Liverpool, Penningtons-Liverpool, Derby, Plymouth, Lowestoft and Caughley factories. The Worcester pattern was used over a span of twenty-five years, and the large number of painters employed to execute the design during that period resulted in a great variation of style, although the arrangement remains amazingly consistent throughout. Large quantities of biscuit and glost wasters were found in the factory site excavations, as discussed in chapter 1. The teapot illustrated is of special interest, as it is inscribed under the base 'W. M. 1766' with a crescent painted above the inscription, all enclosed within an elaborate border ring.

Bowl, 8¼ in. diameter
(Dyson Perrins Museum)

Bowl
Interior pattern

Bowl
Complete pattern

DATE RANGE: 1765–1775

RARITY: Not uncommon

BORDER NOS: 52

MARKS: Open crescent or script 'W'

SHAPES USED: A range of plain thrown and turned bowls, from about $7\frac{1}{4}$ in. to $8\frac{1}{2}$ in. in diameter.

COMMENTARY: This pattern is usually found to be rather sketchily painted, but all of the known examples display a great consistency in the treatment and arrangement of the subject matter. You will see that the pattern on the interior of the bowl bears a strong relationship to that of 'The Promontory Pavilion' (Pattern I.D.1), although obviously done some ten or more years later. Both biscuit and glost wasters of this pattern were uncovered by the factory site excavation, one of which is illustrated by Sandon, along with a completed piece (Plate 24). Spero shows a smaller bowl on page 144.

The Rock Strata Island

*Bowl, 7½ in. diameter
(Dyson Perrins Museum)*

*Bowl
Complete pattern*

DATE RANGE: 1770–1780

RARITY: Common

BORDER NOS: 57

MARKS: Open crescent or script 'W'

SHAPES USED: The pattern can be found on a variety of plain thrown and turned shapes, including the normal range of teawares, but is most often seen on the 5 in. to 7½ in. diameter bowls similar to those illustrated.

COMMENTARY: The Caughley factory made an identical version of this pattern which, when combined with its painted 'C' mark, is very difficult indeed to distinguish from the Worcester version. Lowestoft also used the design as the basis of an underglaze printed pattern; this, too, is quite similar to that of Worcester, but as it is printed rather than painted, should be less of a problem to distinguish. The shape of the window in the principal building in the Worcester design can be either round or square. Numerous biscuit and glost fragments of the design were found in the excavations at the original factory site. Spero illustrates an unusual coffee pot decorated with the pattern (page 116).

The Doughnut Tree

DATE RANGE: 1775–1780

RARITY: Not uncommon

BORDER NOS: 40 on exterior, 20 on exterior base and interior.

MARKS: Open crescent, if any.

SHAPES USED: Convex-fluted, shallow, press-moulded sauceboats, $7\frac{1}{4}$ in. long, elaborately decorated on the exterior.

COMMENTARY: Both the shape of the sauceboat used here, and the elaborately decorated exterior employed reminds one of 'The Full Moon' (Pattern I.B.5) seen earlier. A biscuit fragment of a sauceboat decorated with this design was found in the factory site excavations. We are not aware of any major public collection where an example can be seen, although there are numerous pieces in private collections, both in England and in the United States. Lowestoft had a very similar printed pattern which they used on an almost identical shape (Godden, *Lowestoft Porcelain*, Plate 97).

Sauceboat, $7\frac{1}{4}$ in. long
(Gilbert Bradley Collection)

Sauceboat
Exterior pattern

The Solid Fence Pavilion

DATE RANGE: *c.* 1760

RARITY: Very rare

BORDER NOS: 60

MARKS: Open crescent

SHAPES USED: A large plain thrown and turned coffee cup, 3 in. high and 3 in. in diameter, together with an accompanying saucer of which no complete piece is known.

COMMENTARY: The pattern apparently occurs only on this large cup and its accompanying saucer. The shape of the cup is quite similar to a shape made at Longton Hall, and it is possible that both the shape and the pattern were derived from a Longton Hall precedent. Biscuit fragments of cups decorated with the design were found in the factory site excavations, as was one biscuit fragment of the matching saucer. The Dyson Perrins Museum has an example of the coffee cup, but, as we state above, no complete saucer is known to exist.

Coffee Cup, 3 in. high
(Authors' Collections)

Coffee Cup
Complete pattern

Tureen and Cover, 9 in. diameter
(Sotheby Parke and Bernet and Co.)

Bowl, 6 in. diameter
Reverse pattern (Private Collection)

Mug
Complete pattern

DATE RANGE: *c.* 1754

RARITY: Uncommon

BORDER NOS: Usually none

MARKS: Workmen's marks

SHAPES USED: The pattern can be found on a wide variety of both thrown and turned and press-moulded shapes, including shell-moulded sauceboats, jugs, spreading base mugs, bowls, bell-shaped mugs, cream and milk jugs, dishes, potted meat pots, and tureens and covers similar to that illustrated.

COMMENTARY: As can be seen from a comparison of the photograph of the tureen and cover and the drawing of the mug, there can be a tremendous variation in both the treatment and arrangement of the pattern, some pieces being very stylized and sketchy while others have been painted with great care. Rarely, the pattern is found in company with a reverse design, such as that shown on the bowl illustrated. The painted version of 'The Plantation' was eventually used as the standard for the printed pattern which appeared some years later. (See 'The Plantation Print', Pattern II.B.5). Examples of the pattern can be found in the collections of the Victoria and Albert Museum and of the British Museum.

DATE RANGE: 1751–1755

RARITY: Uncommon

BORDER NOS: 43, 58 or, rarely, 123

MARKS: Workmen's marks

SHAPES USED: Plain thrown and turned shapes, including coffee pots and coffee cans, milk jugs, wet and dry mustard pots, saucers and saucer dishes, and spreading base mugs such as that illustrated.

COMMENTARY: This is the first of a long series of 'fence' patterns at Worcester, found in both its painted and later its printed designs. There will be considerable variation found in the treatment and arrangement of the details of the pattern, although the essential elements are always present. Both biscuit and glost wasters were uncovered by the factory site excavations, and completed examples can be found at the Victoria and Albert Museum.

*Mug, 6½ in. high
(Dyson Perrins Museum)*

Saucer, 4¾ in. diameter
(Gilbert Bradley Collection)

Mug
Complete pattern

DATE RANGE: 1756–1758

RARITY: Very rare

BORDER NOS: None

MARKS: Workmen's marks

SHAPES USED: Press-moulded shapes, including the leaf dish illustrated, $6\frac{3}{4}$ in. long, and a leaf-moulded pickle dish, 5 in. long.

COMMENTARY: This pattern was originally derived from a direct copy of a Chinese porcelain design, being first widely used on Delft and Bow examples, either of which could have been the source of the Worcester pattern. This same original was apparently used also as the source of the three patterns following, Patterns I.D.14, 15, and 16, and is closely related to the design of 'The Picture Scroll Landscape' (Pattern I.B.24) where similar rocks and peony motifs are used but have been adapted to the scroll-moulded shape used with that pattern. When used on pickle dishes, the Oriental emblems of the leaf dish illustrated are omitted due to lack of space. The leaf dish photographed is from the Knowles Boney collection, and was sold by Sotheby's on June 5 1967 (Lot 74).

Leaf Dish, $6\frac{3}{4}$ in. long
(Sotheby Parke Bernet and Co.)

The Leaf Dish Fence

Leaf Dish, 7¼ in. long
(Sotheby Parke Bernet and Co.)

DATE RANGE: 1756–1758

RARITY: Very rare

BORDER NOS: None

MARKS: Workmen's marks

SHAPES USED: A press-moulded leaf dish, 7¼ in. long.

COMMENTARY: This is the first of three patterns (the others being Patterns I.D.15 and 16) which were clearly derived from the design preceding, 'The Chinese Scroll Peony'. The leaf dish illustrated, which is the only example of the pattern known, was sold by Sotheby's on 5 June 1967 (Lot 76) as part of the Knowles Boney collection.

Punch Pot and Cover, 7½ in. high (Gilbert Bradley Collection)

DATE RANGE: 1756–1758

RARITY: Very rare

BORDER NOS: 63 on punch pot illustrated, 61 on octagonal dish

MARKS: Workmen's marks

SHAPES USED: The design is known to have been used on two disparate shapes, one the punch pot and cover illustrated, which is 7½ in. high, the other a press-moulded octagonal dish, 13 in. in length.

COMMENTARY: This is the second of the series of designs which are closely linked with 'The Chinese Scroll Peony' (Pattern I.D.13). As can be seen, the design is carefully and beautifully painted, representing what must be acknowledged as the highest standard of Worcester decoration of this period. The punch pot illustrated is in the private collection of Gilbert Bradley in London. Watney shows the octagonal dish decorated with this pattern in his book on English blue and white porcelain (Plate 28B).

The Prunus Fence

DATE RANGE: 1755–1760

RARITY: Uncommon

BORDER NOS: Usually none

MARKS: Workmen's marks, if any.

SHAPES USED: The pattern will be found on a range of plain thrown and turned shapes as well as some press-moulded lobed pieces, including conical teapots and covers, conical and rounded bowls, spreading base mugs, teabowls and saucers, bowls of various sizes, and a press-moulded lobed teapot of $5\frac{3}{4}$ in. height.

COMMENTARY: This is the last of three designs clearly linked with 'The Chinese Scroll Peony' (Pattern I.D.13) but here we begin to see some relationship with other designs as well, both the earlier 'Zig-Zag Fence' (Pattern I.D.12) as well as the more common 'Prunus Root' (Pattern I.D.27) with which this can be confused. The factory site excavations uncovered several wasters decorated with the pattern, both biscuit and glost. The collection of the British Museum has examples of the pattern. Watney illustrates an interesting conical teapot and conical bowl (Plate 28C).

Saucer, $4\frac{3}{4}$ in. diameter
(Dyson Perrins Museum)

Teabowl
Complete pattern

Bowl, 6¼ in. diameter
(Private Collection)

DATE RANGE: *c.* 1765

RARITY: Very rare

BORDER NOS: None

MARKS: None

SHAPES USED: A plain thrown and turned bowl, 6¼ in. diameter.

COMMENTARY: The only example of this pattern that we have seen is the bowl illustrated, which was brought into the Dyson Perrins Museum some years ago by Anton Gabczewicz, a recognized authority on English porcelains. The design is so closely akin to several patterns known to be of Worcester manufacture that there is little doubt as to its origin.

The Candle Fence

DATE RANGE: 1760–1770

RARITY: Not uncommon

BORDER NOS: 46

MARKS: Open crescent

SHAPES USED: Plain thrown and turned shapes, primarily teawares but also including more unusual pieces such as mustard pots and stands for butter tubs.

COMMENTARY: One can see some points of similarity between this design and that of 'The Peony Fence with Willow' (Pattern I.D.17) preceding, as well as with the two patterns that follow. During the factory site excavations a number of biscuit and glost wasters of the design were found, one of which is illustrated by Sandon (Plate 102), along with a completed bowl of 6 in. diameter.

Coffee Pot and Cover, 9 in. high (Sotheby Parke Bernet and Co.)

Coffee Cup
Complete pattern

The Forked Willow Fence

DATE RANGE: *c.* 1785

RARITY: Very rare

BORDER NOS: 32

MARKS: None

SHAPES USED: The only known example is on the saucer illustrated, a plain thrown and turned shape, $5\frac{1}{3}$ in. diameter, with an added gilt rim.

COMMENTARY: This saucer, which is the only example of a Worcester shape decorated with this pattern known to us, is itself unusual because of its large size and central well, and possibly was intended for use as a stand for an equelle, or broth bowl. The pattern is closely related to 'The Candle Fence' (Pattern I.D.18 preceding), although of a later date. It is a good example of the very detailed painting style to be found at Worcester during this late period of blue and white manufacture.

Saucer, $5\frac{1}{3}$ in. diameter
(Godden Reference Collection)

The Candle Fence Pavilion

Saucer, 5 in. diameter
(Dyson Perrins Museum)

DATE RANGE: 1765–1770

RARITY: Very rare

BORDER NOS: A version of 46

MARKS: Open crescent

SHAPES USED: Teabowls and saucers, the latter usually of 5 in. diameter, all plain thrown and turned shapes.

COMMENTARY: All known examples of this pattern have been 'clobbered' by the addition of polychrome onglaze enamels and gilding. Unlike 'The Question Mark Island' (Pattern I.B.3) this further decoration has been completed several years after the manufacture of the pieces, rather than contemporaneously. You will also find examples of the pattern in the collection of the Victoria and Albert Museum.

Teabowl
Complete pattern

The Landslip

DATE RANGE: 1755–1765

RARITY: Uncommon

BORDER NOS: None

MARKS: Workmen's marks on the earlier pieces, open crescents thereafter.

SHAPES USED: The normal range of plain thrown and turned teawares.

COMMENTARY: This pattern will be found to reflect a considerable variation both in the arrangement of its detail and in the general treatment of its subject matter. The variation will be most apparent on comparison of flatware with a hollow-ware shape. A number of biscuit fragments were found on the site of the original factory during the excavations there, one of these being illustrated by Sandon (Plate 86), along with a completed milk jug decorated with the pattern. Examples can be found in a number of public collections, including that of the Dyson Perrins Museum.

Teapot and Cover, 5 in. high (Authors' Collections)

Teapot Cover Complete pattern

Teapot Complete pattern

The Weeping Willow

Bowl, 5 in. diameter
(Authors' Collections)

Bowl
Complete pattern

DATE RANGE: 1754–1756

RARITY: Very rare

BORDER NOS: None

MARKS: Workmen's marks

SHAPES USED: Plain thrown and turned shapes, including the bowl illustrated, a small teapot and cover, $4\frac{1}{2}$ in. high, and a teabowl and saucer, all indicating that the pattern was probably intended for use on the normal range of teawares.

COMMENTARY: You will see that on the bowl illustrated the central willow tree has been cut off at the rim of the bowl, as was also done on a teabowl waster discovered in the factory site excavations. On the teapot mentioned, in contrast, the willow tree has been completed, as is probably the case on any of the rounded shapes decorated with the pattern. The teapot and cover are owned by a private collector in London.

The Dahlia Rock

DATE RANGE: 1752–1753

RARITY: Very rare

BORDER NOS: None

MARKS: None

SHAPES USED: A plain thrown and turned bowl, $5\frac{1}{4}$ in. diameter.

COMMENTARY: This pattern portrays a very stylized and primitive type of decoration, really unrelated to any other pattern found herein. The colouration is a bright blue, much like that found on 'The Nesting Bird' (Pattern I.C.20). Despite the unique nature of this decoration, the body of the bowl, its shape and other characteristics strongly suggest its Worcester origin.

Bowl, $5\frac{1}{4}$ in. diameter
(Private Collection)

Bowl
Complete pattern

The Hors d'Oeuvres Centre

Star Tray and Waster, 3½ in. diameter
(Godden Reference Collection)

DATE RANGE: 1758–1765

RARITY: Rare

BORDER NOS: 65

MARKS: Workmen's marks on the earlier pieces, perhaps open crescents on those made after 1760.

SHAPES USED: A press-moulded hexagonal star tray, 3½ in. diameter, used as a centre piece in a set of *hors d'oeuvres* trays.

COMMENTARY: This star tray was a part of a set, with six *hors d'oeuvres* trays which fitted around it in a fan pattern to make a circular composition. The trays were decorated with 'The Willow Rock Bird' (Pattern I.C.9), illustrated earlier. The catalogue of the 1979 Albert Amor Exhibition of English Blue and White Soft Paste Porcelains illustrates an assembled, but unmatched set of trays and centrepiece (Item 63). As shown here, biscuit wasters of the shape were found in the factory site excavations, although, oddly enough, none of these had been decorated.

The Bamboo Root

DATE RANGE: *c.* 1755

RARITY: Rare

BORDER NOS: None

MARKS: Workmen's marks, if any.

SHAPES USED: Plain thrown and turned shapes, including teabowls and saucers and coffee cans and cups, some of the latter with 'ear'-shaped handles, as well as a miniature teapot and cover, $3\frac{1}{2}$ in. high.

COMMENTARY: This pattern is a direct copy of a K'ang Hsi original design, and has a close relationship with the somewhat rarer pattern illustrated hereafter ('The Bamboo Peony', Pattern I.D.26). The factory site excavations produced several biscuit and glost fragments decorated with the pattern, sufficient evidence to establish a Worcester origin. We are not aware of any examples in the major public collections, but several pieces are owned by private collectors.

Saucer, $4\frac{3}{4}$ in. diameter
(Gilbert Bradley Collection)

Coffee Can
Complete pattern

The Bamboo Peony

*Coffee Cup, 2⅓ in. high
(Private Collection)*

DATE RANGE : 1754–1755

RARITY : Very rare

BORDER NOS : None

MARKS : None

SHAPES USED : A plain thrown
and turned coffee cup, 2⅓ in. high.

COMMENTARY : This pattern is
linked by its content to the design
preceding ('The Bamboo Root',
Pattern I.D.25), but is entirely
different in its treatment of the
subject matter in the landscape,
and really has no other
relationship. The only known
example of the pattern is on the
coffee cup illustrated.

*Coffee Cup
Complete pattern*

DATE RANGE: 1752–1770

RARITY: Common

BORDER NOS: Usually none

MARKS: Workmen's marks on the earlier pieces, open crescent from roughly 1760 onward.

SHAPES USED: The pattern can be found on both plain thrown and turned pieces as well as with press-moulded, octagonal and fluted shapes, including a full range of teawares, both regularly sized and miniature, a complete range of mugs, serving bowls, mustard pots, etc.

COMMENTARY: The pattern remained popular at the Worcester factory for many years, and, as might be expected, there were notable changes in the quality and style of the painting of it during that period, ranging from the careful work of the 1750s to the poorly executed products of fifteen years later. We have illustrated two bowls which demonstrate the changes which occurred during this time, the conical bowl above being an early example, alongside the rounded bowl below made some fifteen years thereafter. This is another blue and white pattern that can also be found painted onglaze, in this case, in red monochrome. At least three other contemporary English factories used this design, all illustrated by Watney, viz. Lowestoft (Plate 83C), Bow (Plate 18A) and Longton Hall (Plate 41D). Large quantities of both biscuit and glost fragments were found in the waster pits of the original factory during the excavations.

◄ Above: *Bowl, 4¼ in. diameter (Phillips)*
◄ Below: *Bowl, 6 in. diameter (Authors' Collections)*

Saucer
Complete pattern

The Late Rock Floral

Bowl, 7¼ in. diameter
(Authors' Collections)

Bowl
Complete pattern

DATE RANGE: 1780–1785

RARITY: Uncommon

BORDER NOS: 47

MARKS: Open crescent

SHAPES USED: Plain thrown and turned bowls ranging in size from about 7 in. to over 8 in. in diameter.

COMMENTARY: There is little variation to be found in either the treatment or the arrangement of this pattern, the later examples reflecting the crude painting standard and glaring blue colouration associated with many of the 1780s production at the factory. This design is the last, and perhaps the poorest, of a long line of much superior rock and floral patterns. There is an example of the pattern on a bowl owned by the Dyson Perrins Museum.

DATE RANGE: 1775–1780

RARITY: Very rare

BORDER NOS: 41

MARKS: None

SHAPES USED: A press-moulded, lobe-edged meat dish, $8\frac{1}{2}$ in. long.

COMMENTARY: The finely detailed painting which has gone into the example illustrated, along with the inclusion of subject details not frequently seen in other Worcester designs, suggests that this pattern was most probably copied directly from an Oriental original rather than representing some composite from other patterns used at the Worcester factory during this period. The only example of this dish that we have seen was owned by Godden of Worthing Ltd, and we are not aware of its present ownership.

Meat Dish, $8\frac{1}{2}$ in. long
(Godden of Worthing Ltd)

*Teapot and Cover, 5¼ in. high
(Godden Reference Collection)*

DATE RANGE: *c.* 1780

RARITY: Very rare

BORDER NOS: 34

MARKS: None

SHAPES USED: A most unusual press-moulded, square shaped, fluted teapot and cover, 5½ in. high.

COMMENTARY: As indicated, the shape of this teapot and cover is highly unusual, and would not normally be thought to be of Worcester manufacture. However, the body of the pot, its colour and style of decoration, and the shapes of the handle and teapot spout are all evidence of its origin at that factory. Although made at a much later date, the design here is markedly similar to that used in 'The Creeper Print' (Pattern II.B.2) with which this should be compared. The teapot and cover illustrated are the only examples of which we are aware.

I. The Painted Patterns

E. Floral and Fruit

*Sucrier and Cover, 4½ in. high
(Author's Collections)*

*Saucer Dish
Complete pattern*

DATE RANGE: 1757–1780, possibly later.

RARITY: Common

BORDER NOS: 29

MARKS: Workmen's marks on the earlier pieces, open crescent and script 'W' marks thereafter.

SHAPES USED: The pattern is found on a comprehensively large range of plain thrown and turned shapes, primarily teawares.

COMMENTARY: This was an extremely popular pattern, unexacting to paint, and was done by many hands over a very long period of time. Even so, the arrangement tended to remain fairly constant, although the expected variation in treatment did occur. The name of the pattern originated in the twentieth century, when the Worcester factory made a printed version of the earlier painted design. The pattern was used contemporaneously by Bow, Lowestoft, Chaffers and Christians-Liverpool, Plymouth and Derby, and Caughley made a printed version of it as well, so some care must be taken in attributing a particular example to a Worcester origin. Large quantities of both biscuit and glost wasters were found at almost every level of the factory site excavations.

The Butterboat Mansfield

DATE RANGE: 1758–1765

RARITY: Not uncommon

BORDER NOS: None

MARKS: Workmen's marks on earlier examples, open crescents thereafter.

SHAPES USED: Press-moulded butterboats with modelled exteriors, $3\frac{1}{2}$ in. long.

COMMENTARY: The stylistic link to the better known 'Mansfield' (Pattern I.E.1) is immediately evident on comparison of the two, although there are sufficient differences to justify their separate treatment, particularly since 'Mansfield' appears to have been used only on plain thrown and turned shapes. No evidence of the pattern was found in the factory site excavations although a number of wasters of the butterboat shape were discovered.

Butterboat, $3\frac{1}{2}$ in. long (Dyson Perrins Museum)

Butterboat Subsidiary sprays

Butterboat Interior pattern

The Leaf Scroll Border Floral

DATE RANGE: 1760–1765

RARITY: Rare

BORDER NOS: 112

MARKS: Workmen's marks

SHAPES USED: A plain thrown and turned saucer dish, $7\frac{1}{4}$ in. diameter.

COMMENTARY: The only known example of this pattern is on the saucer dish illustrated. It is a further continuation of the 'Mansfield' design (Pattern I.E.1), although again there are sufficient differences to justify distinguishing it as a separate design.

Saucer Dish, $7\frac{1}{4}$ in. diameter
(Gilbert Bradley Collection)

The Big Scroll Border Floral

DATE RANGE: 1758–1760

RARITY: Very rare

BORDER NOS: 119

MARKS: Workmen's marks

SHAPES USED: A press-moulded butterboat or small creamboat, $3\frac{1}{4}$ in. long.

COMMENTARY: This is the last of the series of 'Mansfield' type patterns. The border used with this pattern, which we have shown in greater detail in the tone drawing, appears to be unique to this particular design.

Butterboat, $3\frac{1}{4}$ in. long
(Gilbert Bradley Collection)

Butterboat
Complete pattern

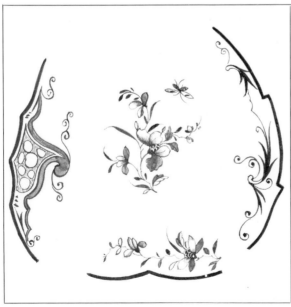

The Reeded Saucer Centre

DATE RANGE: *c.* 1755

RARITY: Very rare

BORDER NOS: 116

MARKS: Workmen's marks

SHAPES USED: A jolleyed reeded saucer, $4\frac{3}{4}$ in. diameter.

COMMENTARY: This example uses a border pattern found as the sole decoration of coffee cans which lack the central spray, and the saucer was obviously intended to accompany these cans. This in itself is unusual, as the Worcester factory did not normally manufacture saucers for use with the reeded coffee cans during this period, but rather produced them solely for use with tea bowls.

Saucer, $4\frac{3}{4}$ in. diameter
(Gilbert Bradley Collection)

DATE RANGE: 1757–1780

RARITY: Common

BORDER NOS: 115

MARKS: Workmen's marks on the earlier pieces, open crescents and script 'W' marks on the later examples.

SHAPES USED: A comprehensive range of press-moulded and jolleyed, feather-moulded and reeded tewares, as well as bowls and 'Blind Earl' type sweetmeat dishes.

COMMENTARY: In the examples made before 1775, there is not a great deal of variation in the arrangement or treatment of the design, but, as can be seen in the comparison of the two coffee pots illustrated, thereafter one will find marked differences as the pattern became more boldly and less carefully painted, typified by the coffee pot on the right. On one known cup and saucer, only the central spray has been used and the subsidiary sprays omitted, but this is a rarely found variation. Large numbers of biscuit and glost fragments of the pattern were found at several levels of the factory site excavations, and completed examples will be included in the collections of most of the major public exhibits of English porcelain.

Left: *Coffee Pot and Cover, 8½ in. high (Authors' Collections)*

Right: *Coffee Pot and Cover, 9¼ in. high (Dyson Perrins Museum)*

Saucer
Complete pattern

*Bowl, 6 in. diameter
(Authors' Collections)*

*Coffee Cup
Complete Pattern*

DATE RANGE: 1765–1775

RARITY: Not uncommon

BORDER NOS: 30 or 31

MARKS: Open crescent and script 'W' marks

SHAPES USED: The pattern was used on a fairly wide range of plain thrown and turned teawares, and is also found, rarely, on a large egg cup, 3 in. high.

COMMENTARY: Border Pattern 31, used frequently with this design, is also found as the sole decoration of blue and white wares, and can also be seen as a border in blue with pieces decorated in polychrome enamels. 'The Peony' pattern was used at Plymouth (see Watney, Plate 93D), but this can be fairly easily distinguished. Caughley made a printed version of the pattern in the 1775–80 period, probably a copy of the Worcester original. A surprisingly large number of biscuit fragments decorated with this design were uncovered in the excavations at the Worcester factory site.

DATE RANGE: 1765–1770

RARITY: Uncommon

BORDER NOS: 34

MARKS: Open crescent

SHAPES USED: A press-moulded sauceboat, around 7 in. long, with an embossed rose pattern on the exterior surface.

COMMENTARY: A biscuit waster of the pattern was found in the factory site excavations. Sandon illustrates the exterior of this sauceboat (Plate 112) although little of the interior design can be seen there. Examples are available for examination in the Dyson Perrins and Victoria and Albert Museums.

Sauceboat, 7 in. long
(Godden Reference Collection)

Bowl, 6 in. diameter
(Authors' Collections)

DATE RANGE: 1765–1770

RARITY: Uncommon

BORDER NOS: 31

MARKS: Open crescent

SHAPES USED: A thrown and turned range of teawares, all with scalloped edges.

COMMENTARY: This would seem to be the only underglaze blue pattern which appears on scallop-edged teawares. There is an obviously strong relationship with 'The Peony' (Pattern I.E.7), although there are significant differences between the two. You should compare this pattern with 'The Early Peony', a printed design (Pattern II.C.4) which is also linked stylistically. A biscuit waster decorated with this border pattern was found in the excavations, although no fragments decorated with the pattern itself were uncovered.

The Cress Dish Floral

DATE RANGE: *c.* 1765

RARITY: Very rare

BORDER NOS: 75, unique to this pattern.

MARKS: Open crescent

SHAPES USED: A jolleyed, pierced cress dish with lobed edges, $7\frac{1}{2}$ in. diameter, presumably with matching dish stand.

COMMENTARY: As far as we know, this is the only hand-painted central design appearing on this particular shape, although cress dishes decorated with the more common transfer-printed designs will be found with hand-painted borders, as a rule.

Cress Dish, $7\frac{1}{2}$ in. diameter
(Gilbert Bradley Collection)

The Egg Cup Floral Sprays

Egg Cup, 2¼ in. high
(Dyson Perrins Museum)

Sprigged Egg Cup, 3 in. high
(Dyson Perrins Museum)

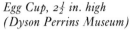

Egg Cup
Complete pattern

DATE RANGE: 1758–1770

RARITY: Rare

BORDER NOS: 32 or 73

MARKS: Workmen's marks on early examples, open crescents thereafter.

SHAPES USED: Thrown and turned egg cups, ranging in size from 2¼ in. to 3 in. in height, sometimes found with 'sprigged' (applied) flowers on the exterior surface.

COMMENTARY: At first glance, it might appear that the floral decoration appearing on the plain egg cup illustrated in the left photograph is different from that on the cup with the applied florets, but on careful examination you will find that the latter design is only a variation of the first, made necessary in order to fit the pattern to the reduced surface area. You will also find that the two border patterns can be used interchangeably with the two shapes decorated. A number of biscuit fragments of these egg cups were found in the factory excavations, one of which is illustrated by Sandon (Plate 92 [left]). A plain example was included in the 1979 Albert Amor Blue and White Exhibition (item 55 in the catalogue).

The Gilliflower/The Narcissus

DATE RANGE: 1770–1785

RARITY: Common

BORDER NOS: 1, 4, 7, 8 or 32

MARKS: Open crescent and script 'W' marks

SHAPES USED: A widely encompassing range of thrown and turned shapes as well as press-moulded pieces, including a complete range of teawares, mugs, leaf trays, shell trays, and asparagus servers as illustrated.

COMMENTARY: This pattern comprises two subjects, the Gilliflower and the Narcissus, which can appear either independently or in conjunction with one another. The subsidiary floral sprays are equally important to the main designs, as they will be found with many other patterns as well as on their own on small items such as eyebaths or pierced eggcups. Caughley also used the Gilliflower as a painted design, and this can be quite easily mistaken for the Worcester version, particularly when found with the Caughley painted 'C' mark. Great quantities of both biscuit and glost fragments of the pattern were found in the excavations. You will see that Worcester also did a printed version of the Gilliflower design which we have called 'The Gilliflower Print' (Pattern II.C.22); for some reason, the factory never produced a transfer-print of the Narcissus pattern.

'Gilliflower' Leaf Tray, 4 in. long
(Authors' Collections)

'Narcissus' Asparagus Server, 3¼ in. long
(Dyson Perrins Museum)

Teapot
Complete pattern

Sauceboat, 7¼ in. long
(Dyson Perrins Museum)

DATE RANGE: 1770–1780

RARITY: Not uncommon

BORDER NOS: 7 and/or 34

MARKS: Open crescent

SHAPES USED: A variety of both thrown and turned and press-moulded shapes, including sauceboats, as illustrated, sweetmeat stands, ink wells, and a full range of miniature tewares, the teapot illustrated being one of these.

COMMENTARY: This pattern falls within the group of central floral motifs which are used in conjunction with 'The Gilliflower' and 'The Narcissus' designs, sharing with these patterns the same subsidiary sprays (see Pattern I.E.12, preceding). Where

space on the shape decorated permitted, the main spray can be painted in a more elaborate manner, as illustrated by the sauceboat pictured here. Examples of the pattern are included in the collections of the Dyson Perrins and Victoria and Albert Museums.

Miniature Teapot, 3 in. high
(Authors' Collections)

The Fruit Sprays

Left: *Mug, 3¼ in. high*
Right: *Coffee Cup, 2½ in. high*
(Dyson Perrins Museum)

DATE RANGE: 1775–1785

RARITY: Not uncommon

BORDER NOS: 7 or 8

MARKS: Open crescent

SHAPES USED: A range of plain thrown and turned teawares, together with a more unusual group of press-moulded, fluted teawares and plain thrown and turned cylinder mugs.

COMMENTARY: The painting style displayed on pieces decorated with this pattern can vary enormously, as can be seen by comparing the earlier mug illustrated with the coffee cup made some ten years later. The subsidiary sprigs found with this design are often the same as those associated with the 'Gilliflower/ Narcissus' or the 'Rose' preceding (Patterns I.E.12 and 13). Many of the public collections of English porcelain will have examples of this pattern.

*Teapot and Cover, 6 in. high
(Godden Reference Collection)*

DATE RANGE: *c.* 1785

RARITY: Very rare

BORDER NOS: 10

MARKS: Open crescent

SHAPES USED: A plain thrown and turned teapot and cover with rosebud knop, overall height 6 in.

COMMENTARY: This pattern displays a highly stylized form of painting, quite unlike Worcester in treatment and most likely derived from a pattern first made at the Caughley factory. The shape of the pot confirms that the Worcester standard of potting was still being maintained at this late date, but the quality and style of the painting itself is quite appalling.

The Caughley Floral Sprays

Coffee Cup, 2½ in. high
(Dyson Perrins Museum)

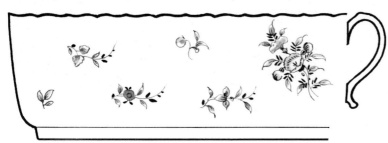

Coffee Cup
Complete pattern

DATE RANGE: *c.* 1785

RARITY: Very rare

BORDER NOS: 13

MARKS: Open crescent

SHAPES USED: A jolleyed coffee
cup with moulded handle, 2½ in.
high, together with a complete
range of dessertwares.

COMMENTARY: The shape of the
cup upon which this pattern
appears was copied from those
manufactured in some quantity by
the Caughley factory (themselves
copying Chinese export ware),
and the style of painting was
similarly 'borrowed', all obviously
aimed at passing off the Worcester
pieces for those made by its
principal competitor. Although we
have not seen the exact design on
Caughley examples, it would not
be surprising to find that this, too,
was filched by Worcester. It is not
known whether the gilt border on
the cup was applied at the factory
or was added by Chamberlain
thereafter. The only known
example of this pattern in a public
collection is the coffee cup
illustrated, but, on April 15 1980,
Sotheby Parke Bernet, New York
sold a complete dessertware
service which was decorated with
this design.

The Late Floral Bouquet

*Coffee Cup, 2½ in. high
(Authors' Collections)*

DATE RANGE: *c.* 1785

RARITY: Very rare

BORDER NOS: 13

MARKS: Open crescent

SHAPES USED: A jolleyed coffee cup with fluted exterior, 2½ in. high.

COMMENTARY: Although no evidence of the Worcester origin of this pattern was produced through the factory site excavations, the shape of the coffee cup and the characteristics which it displays leaves little doubt as to its place of manufacture. Unfortunately, neither the potting nor the decoration of this particular piece can be said to add to the reputation of the Worcester factory; indeed it is a striking example of the shabby state in which the factory found itself only a decade after the departure of Dr Wall. The gilding on the cup was possibly added by Chamberlain, who purchased some part of the factory's production during this period.

The Cornucopia Floral

Cornucopia, 9 in. long
(Godden Reference Collection)

Cornucopia
Complete pattern

DATE RANGE: 1755–1760

RARITY: Uncommon

BORDER NOS: 19

MARKS: Workmen's marks

SHAPES USED: Press-moulded cornucopias, usually 9 in. to $9\frac{1}{2}$ in. in length.

COMMENTARY: There are tremendous variations in both style and arrangement to be seen in comparing any two examples of these cornucopias, and great care must be taken to assure that any example can be attributed to this particular pattern rather than one of the other two cornucopia patterns that follow (Patterns I.E.19 and 20). However, only a few of Worcester's rival factories produced cornucopias of this particular shape, and it is comparatively easy to identify a piece as being of Worcester origin. Examples of the pattern can also be seen at the Dyson Perrins Museum.

DATE RANGE: *c.* 1760

RARITY: Very rare

BORDER NOS: 114

MARKS: None

SHAPES USED: A press-moulded cornucopia, about 9 in. long.

COMMENTARY: The only example we have seen of this rare pattern was brought into Wolfe's Antiques at Droitwich several years ago, from which the tone drawing was taken. The present whereabouts of this piece is unknown to us, but based on its shape and body, there is little doubt in our minds of its Worcester origin. It can easily be confused with the design of the preceding pattern, 'The Cornucopia Floral' (Pattern I.E.18), whose style and arrangement can vary considerably, even to approaching the arrangement of this quite distinct design.

Cornucopia
Full pattern

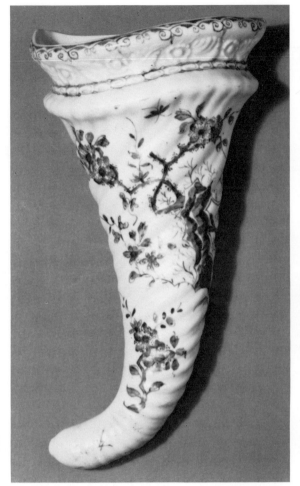
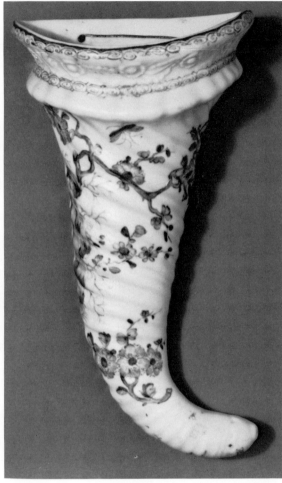

Pair, Cornucopias, 11 in. long
(Venner's Antiques)

DATE RANGE: 1757–1760

RARITY: Uncommon

BORDER NOS: 17 and 22

MARKS: Workmen's marks and pseudo-Meissen crossed-sword marks

SHAPES USED: Press-moulded cornucopias, ranging in size from 9 in. to about 11 in. long.

COMMENTARY: This is probably the most common of the cornucopia patterns and several examples have been seen including one in the Godden Reference Collection; Barrett illustrates another (Plate 45B). For some reason yet unknown, it is not unusual to find these cornucopias with several workmen's marks on the same piece. The same style of design can be found on 'The Prunus Branch Bird' (Pattern I.C.13).

Jug
Full pattern

◄ *Jug, 11¼ in. high*
(Dyson Perrins Museum)

DATE RANGE: 1755–1760

RARITY: Uncommon

BORDER NOS: None

MARKS: Workmen's marks or pseudo-Meissen crossed sword marks.

SHAPES USED: Press-moulded, cabbage-leaf jugs, with and without mask spouts, 8 in. to 11¼ in. high, some with elaborately moulded handles.

COMMENTARY: Bearing in mind the difference in size of the jugs decorated with this design, there is a remarkable consistency in the arrangement of the pattern and in the treatment of the subject matter, making this one of the easiest of the Worcester floral patterns to recognize. Spero shows a somewhat smaller jug (page 127), and Severne Mackenna pictures the smallest of these (Plate 10 [20]).

The Bluebell Spray

DATE RANGE: *c.* 1765

RARITY: Very rare

BORDER NOS: 4

MARKS: None

SHAPES USED: A press-moulded, shell-shaped dish, probably intended for use as a sweetmeat tray, 4⅘ in. diameter.

COMMENTARY: The flower sprays pictured in this pattern, as any home gardener will quickly recognize, are completely imaginary, and are only a composite of wild flowers growing in the Worcester area at the time. Nevertheless, although not the first, this pattern marks the introduction of a new and 'natural' style of flower painting at the factory, probably inspired by the floral engravings found in pattern and botanical books of that period. This rare example was formerly in the Knowles Boney collection, and was sold on 30 January 1980 in the Phillips's saleroom in London. Similar shell-shaped dishes were made by the Worcester factory some years later, and were decorated with underglaze blue transfer-prints. See 'The Primula' and 'The Marrow' printed designs (Patterns II.C.21 and II.B.24) for examples of these.

Shell Dish, 4⅘ in. diameter
(Authors' Collections)

The Broth Bowl Floral Sprays

Broth Bowl Stand, 7 in. diameter
(Godden Reference Collection)

DATE RANGE: 1760–1765

RARITY: Rare

BORDER NOS: None

MARKS: Workmen's marks on earliest examples, open crescents thereafter.

SHAPES USED: A jolleyed broth bowl (or equelle), cover and stand, the latter of 7 in. diameter.

COMMENTARY: Most of the known examples of this pattern have had the floral sprays filled in with coloured enamels heightened with gold, and have an added yellow border. While this re-colouring process is normally thought of as 'clobbering', it is quite conceivable that the colouration in this case was a contemporary and deliberate factory decoration. Another example of a bowl and stand is owned by the Dyson Perrins Museum.

The Honeysuckle, Narcissus and Anemone Spray I.E.24

DATE RANGE: 1760–1765

RARITY: Uncommon

BORDER NOS: None

MARKS: Open crescent, if any.

SHAPES USED: Pierced circular baskets, $7\frac{3}{4}$ in. to 8 in. diameter, with applied exterior florets.

COMMENTARY: This pattern, which only appears on pierced baskets of the kind illustrated, is notable primarily for the very finely painted design, which shows virtually no variation from example to example, possibly due to the use of some kind of tracing stencil to assure consistency. It is frequently listed, by both sale rooms and dealers, as being a printed pattern, and only the most careful examination will prove that it was, indeed, painted. To our knowledge, none of the major public porcelain collections own an example of this pattern.

Basket, $7\frac{3}{4}$ in. diameter
(Sotheby Parke Bernet and Co.)

The Heavy Naturalistic Floral

Jug, 8 in. high
(Authors' Collections)

DATE RANGE: 1760–1765

RARITY: Uncommon

BORDER NOS: None

MARKS: Workmen's marks on the earliest examples, open crescents thereafter.

SHAPES USED: Press-moulded, cabbage-leaf jugs, both with and without mask spouts, usually around 8 in. high, sometimes with an elaborate moulded handle.

COMMENTARY: The flaccid painting of this pattern bears some resemblance to engraved prints found in *The Ladies' Amusement* and similar publications of that day, and may well have been copied directly from one of these. The consistency of the painting, always meticulously done, suggests that like the previous design (Pattern I.E.24), some kind of stencil outline may have been used to assure a lack of variation. It is interesting to speculate why Worcester continued to produce elaborate floral paintings of this style when printed versions were surely available at a lower per unit cost. Biscuit fragments decorated with this pattern were found in the factory site excavations, and a complete example can be seen at the Dyson Perrins Museum.

Jug
Reverse pattern

Jug
Front pattern

DATE RANGE: 1760–1765

RARITY: Rare

BORDER NOS: None

MARKS: Open crescent

SHAPES USED: A press-moulded, overlapping cabbage-leaf dish, 13¾ in. or 10¼ in. long, with cross-stem handle, and pickle trays, 3½ in. long.

COMMENTARY: This is the first of a series of 'heavy' naturalistic patterns which feature a central flower past its prime, or as we have described it, in a 'blown' stage of development. Compare the two patterns following (I.E.27 and 28) to see the strong similarity in painting content and style. The leaf dish illustrated was sold by Christie's on 21 April 1969 (Lot 32), and we are unaware of its present ownership. An example in the Victoria and Albert Museum of the same shape, but smaller, is decorated with only a single tulip in its centre, presumably due to the comparative lack of space. Another of the 'single tulip' variations can be found on a pickle tray, 3½ in. long, in the authors' collections.

Leaf Dish, 13¾ in. long (Christie, Manson and Woods Ltd)

The Blown Peony Wall Pocket

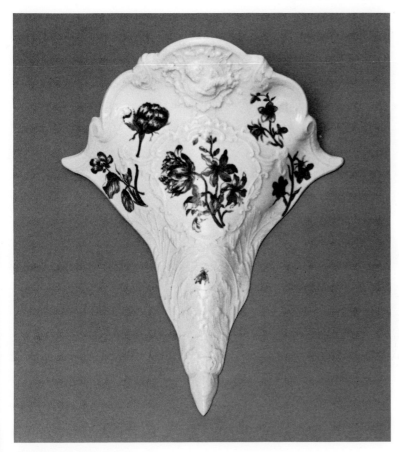

DATE RANGE: 1760–1765

RARITY: Rare

BORDER NOS: None

MARKS: None

SHAPES USED: A press-moulded wall pocket (or wall vase), $8\frac{1}{4}$ in. in length.

COMMENTARY: This design appears on a very unusual and quite rare Worcester shape, most often found with a polychrome onglaze decoration. The painting on this piece, again featuring a 'blown' flower as its central motif, is a continuation of the series of 'heavy' naturalistic painting. The wall pocket illustrated was featured in the Albert Amor Exhibition of English Blue and White Porcelain in 1979, Catalogue Number 65.

Wall Pocket, $8\frac{1}{4}$ in. long
(Albert Amor Ltd)

The Blown Rose Leaf Tray

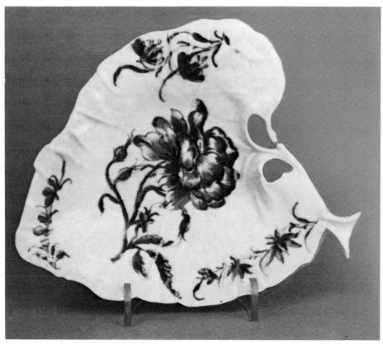

Leaf Tray, 5½ in. long
(Albert Amor Ltd)

DATE RANGE: 1760–1765

RARITY: Rare

BORDER NOS: None

MARKS: Open crescent

SHAPES USED: A press-moulded leaf tray, shaped as a dock-leaf with short stock handle, 5½ in. long.

COMMENTARY: This is the last of the line of 'heavy' blown floral designs illustrated here. We believe it quite possible that there are other similar patterns featuring a different 'blown' floral motif which we have not seen. The style of the painting is the distinctive characteristic of this group, and should make it easy to identify other examples of Worcester origin. The leaf tray illustrated was Catalogue Number 60 in the 1979 Albert Amor Exhibition. Another example of this pattern can be seen in the collection of the Victoria and Albert Museum.

The Ashmolean Candlestick

DATE RANGE: *c.* 1760

RARITY: Very rare

BORDER NOS: None

MARKS: None

SHAPES USED: Press-moulded candlesticks of silver shape, with gadroon moulding, $9\frac{1}{2}$ in. high.

COMMENTARY: The only known examples of this pattern are on a pair of candlesticks, one of which is illustrated. Rissik Marshall illustrates one of these (Plate 43[888]) as well.

Candlestick, $9\frac{1}{2}$ in. high
(The Ashmolean Museum, Oxford)

Porringer, 5$\frac{1}{2}$ in. diameter
(Dyson Perrins Museum)

Fork Handle, 2$\frac{3}{4}$ in. long
(Dyson Perrins Museum)

Leaf Tray, 3⅞ in. long
(Authors' Collections)

DATE RANGE: 1758–1760

RARITY: Uncommon

BORDER NOS: None

MARKS: Workmen's marks, if any

SHAPES USED: The pattern was used on a variety of shapes, including press-moulded leaf trays, pistol-grip knife and fork handles, and thrown and turned porringers with moulded handles, all as illustrated.

COMMENTARY: This design marks a subtle shift from the flaccid painting which we have seen in the preceding patterns toward a slightly more formalistic and less natural style. As you will see, this becomes more and more pronounced in later decades. Although the shapes decorated with the design cover an extreme range, a careful examination will confirm that the pattern on each is the same. Examples of several of the different shapes decorated with this pattern can be found at the Dyson Perrins Museum in Worcester.

*Sweetmeat Stand, 5½ in. high,
8⅜ in. diameter
(Dyson Perrins Museum)*

DATE RANGE: 1765–1770

RARITY: Rare

BORDER NOS: 42 on sweetmeat
stand, 4 on dish

MARKS: Usually none

SHAPES USED: Press-moulded,
modelled and assembled
sweetmeat stand, 5½ in. high and
8⅜ in. in diameter, consisting of
four shell dishes on two tiers, all
mounted on a base of small shells
and seaweed. A part of the pattern
also was used on a press-moulded,
overlapping leaf dish, 11 in. in
diameter.

COMMENTARY: We are now
beginning to see the clear
emergence of the formalistic style
of painting, here very precise and
detailed as though pencilled. It is
somewhat unusual to find the
central design of the more
comprehensive shell stand (where
the entire pattern is used) being
employed in the moulded dish,
and it may well be that this same
rose motif was also used on other
shapes that we have not seen. The
sweetmeat stand is part of the
collection at the Dyson Perrins
Museum, and another view of it
was illustrated by Sandon (Plate
123). The moulded dish was in
the Jenkins Collection sale at
Sotheby's on 28 April 1970
(Lot 84).

Moulded Dish, 11 in. diameter
(Sotheby Parke Bernet and Co.)

▲ *Leaf Dish, 9 in. long*
(Authors' Collections)

▼ *Leaf Dish, 7¾ in. long*
(Gilbert Bradley Collection)

DATE RANGE: 1765–1770

RARITY: Uncommon

BORDER NOS: 4

MARKS: Open crescent, if any.

SHAPES USED: A variety of press-moulded single or double vine-leaf dishes with twig handles, ranging in size from 6 in. to 9 in. length.

COMMENTARY: A casual glance at the two leaf dishes illustrated would raise doubts as to whether they were really the same pattern of decoration, but a closer look will show that the sprays are virtually identical, although located in different positions on the face of the pieces. Therefore, you must expect to find a very considerable variation in the arrangement of this pattern as well as some differences in painting style. Another piece with the same design, again differently arranged, was included in the 1979 Albert Amor Exhibition, Catalogue Number 20.

The Ladle Sprays

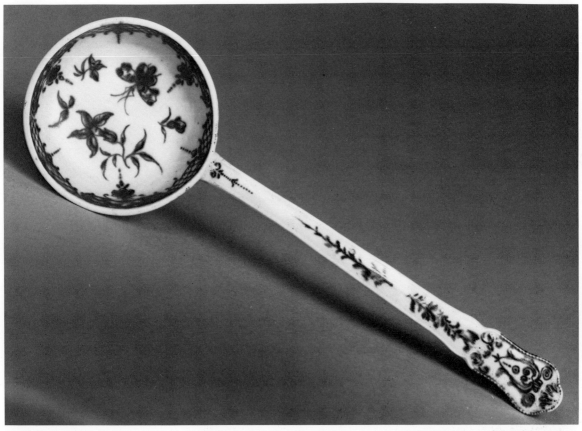

Ladle, 8 in. long
(Dyson Perrins Museum)

DATE RANGE: 1765–1770

RARITY: Very rare

BORDER NOS: 76

MARKS: None

SHAPES USED: A press-moulded ladle, 8 in. long.

COMMENTARY: The Worcester origin of this very unusual piece can only be established through its physical characteristics, including the body of the ladle, the style of painting, and the shape itself, which is known on identically sized ladles decorated with polychrome onglaze enamels. The only known example having an underglaze blue decoration is the piece illustrated.

DATE RANGE: 1765–1775

RARITY: Rare

BORDER NOS: None

MARKS: Open crescent

SHAPES USED: Press-moulded, heavily modelled, chamber candlesticks, 5 in. to 6 in. diameter.

COMMENTARY: On the examples we have seen, there has been very little variation in the arrangement of the sprays, although there are some noticeable differences in the way the design has been treated by the different hands that painted it. Several biscuit fragments decorated with the pattern were found in the factory site excavations; Sandon illustrates one of these (Plate 97) and Hobson also illustrates the design (Plate XIX, bottom centre). Candlesticks can be seen at several of the major public collections, including the British Museum and the Victoria and Albert Museum.

Chamber Candlestick, 5 in. diameter
(Dyson Perrins Museum)

The Junket Dish Florals

DATE RANGE: 1760–1775

RARITY: Uncommon

BORDER NOS: 32 or 113, depending on the shape of the dish.

MARKS: Open crescent

SHAPES USED: Press-moulded junket dishes with various moulded surfaces, usually around 9 in. to $9\frac{1}{2}$ in. diameter.

COMMENTARY: There is variation in this pattern, partly because of the differences in the moulding used on the dishes on which it is found, and partly because of the way in which the sprays have been arranged and painted on the different surfaces. In some examples you will find crisply painted sprays, while in others such heavy washes of colour have been used that the subject line is almost completely obliterated. We have illustrated two dishes with different moulding, one of which has a plain centre upon which a carnation has been painted, and the other with a moulded centre where the painter has simply decorated the already raised lines. Exact copies of these dishes were made by the Chinese factories, who even used the Worcester crescent mark, so some caution is advisable here. Biscuit fragments of this shape and pattern were commonly found during the factory site excavations.

Top: *Junket Dish, $9\frac{1}{4}$ in. diameter (Phillips)*
Left: *Junket Dish, 9 in. diameter (Authors' Collections)*

Bowl, 8 in. diameter
(Godden of Worthing Ltd)

DATE RANGE: *c.* 1760

RARITY: Rare

BORDER NOS: 49 or 50

MARKS: Workmen's marks or open crescent.

SHAPES USED: A jolleyed bowl, 8 in. diameter.

COMMENTARY: The inside of this bowl is decorated with a variation of one of the designs used in 'The Fisherman and Willow Pavilion' (Pattern I.B.21), and this could be equally well classified as a landscape with figure rather than as a floral. However, it is the exterior design which we consider of primary interest, and have placed it accordingly. We have seen two identical bowls decorated with this pattern, both owned by Godden of Worthing Ltd, and biscuit fragments of the design were uncovered during the factory site excavations, leaving no doubt as to its Worcester origin.

The Strap Flute Sauceboat Floral

DATE RANGE: 1770–1780

RARITY: Common

BORDER NOS: 32

MARKS: Open crescent

SHAPES USED: Press-moulded strap-fluted sauceboats, ranging in size from $6\frac{1}{4}$ in. to $7\frac{3}{4}$ in. in length.

COMMENTARY: Over the decade of its manufacture the pattern was apparently painted by a large number of hands, and one will find a very great disparity in both the arrangement and treatment of the design, as can readily be seen through a comparison of the two examples shown here. The sauceboat illustrated by Sandon (Plate 99) shows yet another variation of the same basic theme. Therefore, great care must be exercised in attempting to identify this pattern, although the shape and fluting of the sauceboat on which it appears will prove to be the most reliable guide. You will notice that the subsidiary sprigs used on both of the illustrated examples are closely related to those of 'The Gilliflower/ Narcissus' group (Pattern I.E.12). Numerous wasters, both biscuit and glost, were found in the excavations decorated with the many variations of this popular pattern.

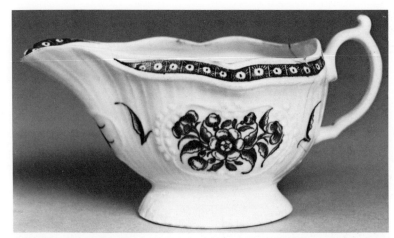

*Sauceboat, $6\frac{1}{4}$ in. long
(Dyson Perrins Museum)*

*Sauceboat, $6\frac{1}{4}$ in. long
(Dyson Perrins Museum)*

Butterboat, 3¼ in. long
(Dyson Perrins Museum)

DATE RANGE: *c.* 1770

RARITY: Uncommon

BORDER NOS: 32

MARKS: Open crescent

SHAPES USED: A press-moulded, leaf-shaped butterboat, 3¼ long.

COMMENTARY: No factory wasters decorated with this precise pattern were found in the site excavations at Worcester, although several fragments of identical shape were uncovered there. The butterboat illustrated was damaged some years ago and has since been restored and partly repainted, as can be seen. Sandon illustrates the exterior of the butterboat (Plate 110), along with a waster of its shape.

The Chelsea Ewer Sprays

*Creamboat, 3⅜ in. long
(Authors' Collections)*

DATE RANGE: *c.* 1770

RARITY: Rare

BORDER NOS: 5 at base

MARKS: Open crescent

SHAPES USED: Press-moulded, heavily modelled 'Chelsea ewer' type creamboats, around 3⅜ in. long.

COMMENTARY: The creamboat illustrated is of a shape frequently used at the Worcester factory during this period. They occur in two sizes, one taller than the other (see 'The Trellis Scroll Border Floral', Pattern I.E.45 for an example of the taller version). The Caughley factory also used a creamboat very similar to this shape, and the Chamberlain records frequently refer to it as a 'Chelsea ewer', possibly because of a similar shape first made at that London factory.

Butter Tub and Cover, $5\frac{1}{4}$ in. long (Sotheby Parke Bernet and Co.)

DATE RANGE: *c.* 1760

RARITY: Very rare

BORDER NOS: None

MARKS: Open crescent

SHAPES USED: A jolleyed and press-moulded butter tub and cover with an unusual apple knop, $5\frac{1}{2}$ in. long.

COMMENTARY: The running sprays used on this buttertub are found primarily as borders and subsidiary decorations on the larger shapes such as tureens, as well as on smaller pieces like this buttertub and cover. The piece illustrated was sold by Sotheby's as part of the Jenkins Collection on 28 April 1970 (Lot 57), and is now owned by the Godden Reference Collection, Worthing.

The Pickle Leaf Daisy

DATE RANGE: 1758–1765

RARITY: Not uncommon

BORDER NOS: None

MARKS: Workmen's marks or open crescent

SHAPES USED: Press-moulded butterboats (or pickle boats) with twig handle and heavily-modelled 'geranium leaf' exteriors, 3 in. long, and press-moulded leaf trays, $5\frac{1}{2}$ in. long, both as illustrated.

COMMENTARY: As can be seen in the illustrations, some variation will be found in the arrangement of the pattern, with a simple blue line along the border of the larger of the two shapes. Biscuit wasters of both shapes were found in the factory site excavations, and several complete examples can be seen in many of the major public porcelain collections.

Above: *Leaf Tray, $5\frac{1}{2}$ in. long (Dyson Perrins Museum)*

Right: *Butterboat, 3 in. long (Authors' Collections)*

*Leaf Tray, $3\frac{1}{2}$ in. long
(Authors' Collections)*

DATE RANGE: 1758–1770

RARITY: Common

BORDER NOS: 4

MARKS: Workmen's marks on the earlier pieces, open crescents thereafter.

SHAPES USED: Press-moulded vine-leaf trays, usually $3\frac{1}{2}$ in. to 4 in. in length.

COMMENTARY: The treatment of this design can and does vary tremendously, particularly noticeable when comparing a very early piece, such as the leaf tray illustrated, with another made a decade later. Nevertheless, over the years, the basic arrangement remained surprisingly constant. You may wish to compare the leaf tray above with those illustrated by Sandon (Plate 109) and Spero (page 150) to see the stylistic variation in the pattern. Quantities of biscuit and glost fragments were found in the waster pits on the factory site during several of the excavations. Caughley made a printed version of this pattern some years later, but it should be easily distinguishable.

The Knife Handle Formal Daisy

DATE RANGE: 1760–1765

RARITY: Not uncommon

BORDER NOS: None

MARKS: Usually none

SHAPES USED: Press-moulded, pistol-grip knife and fork handles, 3 in. to 5 in. in length.

COMMENTARY: The design is taken from a style of painting usually attributed to St Cloud and other French porcelain factories, although this pattern apparently is not a direct copy of any of those. A number of biscuit fragments of knife handles decorated with this pattern were found in the excavations, one illustrated by Sandon (Plate 89).

Pair, Knife Handles, $3\frac{3}{4}$ in. long (Private Collection)

*Knife Handle
Front pattern*

*Knife Handle
Side pattern*

The Knife Handle Formal Floral

DATE RANGE: 1760–1765

RARITY: Uncommon

BORDER NOS: None

MARKS: Usually none

SHAPES USED: Press-moulded, pistol-grip knife and fork handles, usually 3 in. to 4 in. in length.

COMMENTARY: This design is not as frequently seen as that preceding (Pattern I.E.43), and again was derived from the style of decoration used by the St Cloud factory and other contemporary French manufacturers. Although no wasters decorated with this pattern were found in the factory site excavations, the shape of the handles and the similarity in style to the authenticated 'Knife Handle Formal Daisy' design leave little doubt of its Worcester origin.

Fork Handle, 3¼ in. long
(Private Collection)

Knife Handle
Front pattern

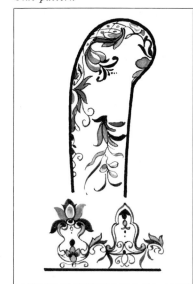

Knife Handle
Side pattern

The Trellis Scroll Border Floral

DATE RANGE: *c.* 1770

RARITY: Very rare

BORDER NOS: 5 at base

MARKS: Open crescent

SHAPES USED: Press-moulded, heavily modelled, 'Chelsea ewer' type creamboats of the taller shape, $4\frac{1}{2}$ in. long and $3\frac{1}{2}$ in. high.

COMMENTARY: While we have tried to avoid making value judgements as to the desirability of any design, it is obvious that this pattern is artistically unbalanced, with a massive 'busy' decoration on one side of the creamboat and a simple floral sprig on the other, leading one to wonder if this incongruity may have contributed to its lack of appeal and thus to the rarity of the pattern. The shape is an example of the taller 'Chelsea ewer' made at Worcester, the smaller version being seen previously in 'The Chelsea Ewer Sprays' (Pattern I.E.39). The Lowestoft factory made an almost exact copy of this design which they used on a very similar shape, an example of which can be seen at the Godden Reference Collection along with a Worcester example.

*Creamboat, $4\frac{1}{2}$ in. long
(Gilbert Bradley Collection)*

*Creamboat
Complete pattern*

Cream Jug, 2½ in. high
(Private Collection)

DATE RANGE: *c.* 1765

RARITY: Rare

BORDER NOS: None

MARKS: Open crescent

SHAPES USED: Thrown and turned, barrel-shaped cream jugs with shaped exterior grooves, ranging from 2½ in. to 3½ in. in height, and having either moulded or grooved handles.

COMMENTARY: This barrel shape is more frequently found with polychrome onglaze decoration, and it is unusual to see it in the underglaze blue. Watney illustrates a jug slightly larger than that illustrated here (Plate 34C) and another of that same size was included in the 1979 Albert Amor Exhibition as Catalogue Number 44. Several wasters with the identical shape of this cream jug were found in the excavations, but none of these was decorated with this particular design. A similar pattern on an identical shape was used at Lowestoft (see Godden, *Lowestoft Porcelain*, Plate 91).

DATE RANGE: *c.* 1775

RARITY: Uncommon

BORDER NOS: 3

MARKS: It has its own unique mark, as illustrated.

SHAPES USED: A range of press-moulded dessertwares, including a lobed circular dish, scallop-shell dishes like that illustrated, oval-, heart-, and square-shaped dishes, and sauce tureens with covers and stands.

COMMENTARY: The Bow factory made a very similar pattern, possibly some years before the Worcester version emerged, and this pattern is often mistakenly described as of Bow manufacture. However, there are marked differences between the two, and there should be no real difficulty in distinguishing them. Although examples of the pattern are owned by several private collectors, we are not aware of a piece decorated with this design in any of the major public collections.

Shell Dish, 8 in. long
(Gilbert Bradley Collection)

Mark

The Blind Earl

DATE RANGE: *c.* 1765

RARITY: Rare

BORDER NOS: None

MARKS: Open crescent, if any.

SHAPES USED: Press-moulded plates and sweetmeat dishes of the 'Blind Earl' design, with modelled rose bush branches, leaves and buds, and scalloped edges. The plates are usually $7\frac{3}{4}$ in. to 8 in. in diameter, and the sweetmeat dishes are about $5\frac{3}{4}$ in. to 6 in. long.

COMMENTARY: The pattern, as can be seen, is basically coloured over the raised moulding of the shape, with insects or other details added by free-hand painting. Tradition has it that the shape was named after the Earl of Coventry who had lost his sight as the result of a hunting accident, and subsequently asked the Worcester factory to make a set of porcelain that could be felt as well as seen. Appealing as this story may be, it is only folklore, as the excavations definitely establish that the pattern was in production at Worcester for several years prior to the Earl's unfortunate accident.

An almost complete biscuit waster of a plate was found in the excavations, and the sweetmeat dish is illustrated by both Watney (Plate 36B) and Spero (page 138).

Plate, $7\frac{3}{4}$ in. diameter (Sotheby Parke Bernet and Co.)

The Chrysanthemum

DATE RANGE: 1757–1775

RARITY: Common

BORDER NOS: 48

MARKS: Workmen's marks on earlier pieces, open crescents thereafter.

SHAPES USED: Either press-moulded or jolleyed flatware and teaware, including all of the basic shapes together with teapot stands and spoon trays.

COMMENTARY: The decoration of this 'chrysanthemum-moulded' ware is very dependent upon the actual moulding used on the individual pieces, and can vary substantially. The most common variation, illustrated here, involves a moulded frieze of flowers surrounding a painted chrysanthemum centre. On other examples, usually hollow-ware pieces, the painted chrysanthemum centre is omitted and replaced by an inner border design. A third variation found on oval shapes, retains the central painted chrysanthemum, but adds a leaf emerging from the side of the flower. The outer lambrequin border pattern can quite commonly be found on its own with reeded-shape tewares. Caughley used the Chrysanthemum as a printed pattern, but added washes of colour to it, making it quite difficult to distinguish in some cases.

Saucer Dish, $6\frac{3}{4}$ in. diameter (Dyson Perrins Museum)

*Teabowl and Saucer, 4¾ in.
diameter
(Sotheby Parke Bernet and Co.)*

DATE RANGE: 1758–1760

RARITY: Very rare

BORDER NOS: 48

MARKS: Workmen's marks

SHAPES USED: A jolleyed
teabowl and saucer, the latter of
around 4¾ in. diameter, of the
'chrysanthemum' design.

COMMENTARY: The only known
example of this unusual pattern
was sold as a part of the Jenkins
Collection at Sotheby's on 28
April 1970 (Lot 97). It is an
obvious variant of the common
'Chrysanthemum' (Pattern
I.E.49), with the more usual
flower replaced with a painted
anemone; otherwise the two are
identical, with the same
lambrequin border design.

The Floral Swag, Ribbon and Scroll

Coffee Can, $2\frac{5}{8}$ in. high
(Dyson Perrins Museum)

DATE RANGE: *c.* 1755

RARITY: Very rare

BORDER NOS: None

MARKS: Workmen's marks

SHAPES USED: A plain, cylindrical, thrown and turned coffee can, $2\frac{5}{8}$ in. high, with slightly spreading base.

COMMENTARY: The only known example of this very rare design is the coffee can illustrated. The shape of the coffee can is often referred to as a 'scratch cross' type, as some of these early pieces were marked on the base by an incised line or cross, the meaning of which is unknown.

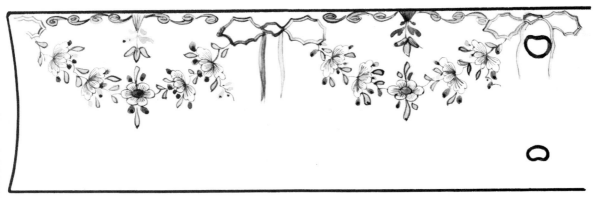

Coffee Can
Complete pattern

DATE RANGE: *c.* 1780

RARITY: Uncommon

BORDER NOS: I

MARKS: An imitation Chantilly 'hunting horn', as illustrated.

SHAPES USED: Press-moulded teawares, including the teapot and cover, $5\frac{1}{2}$ in. high, and the teapot stand, $5\frac{1}{2}$ in. diameter, illustrated.

COMMENTARY: This pattern is a direct copy of a design used extensively by the Chantilly factory in France, and the simultaneous use by the Worcester enterprise of the Chantilly mark necessarily leads to the conclusion that the English company had every intention of misleading an unsuspecting buyer as to the origin of the wares decorated with this design. Worcester's main rival during this period, the Caughley factory, also made the pattern but without the hunting horn mark, so there seemed to be a procession of 'borrowing' in this instance. The pattern was usually embellished with a bright gold edging which is particularly prominent. Other examples of the design are owned by several private collectors.

Teapot, Cover and Stand, $5\frac{1}{2}$ in. high
(Dyson Perrins Museum)

Mark

The Flower Head and Leaf Band

DATE RANGE: 1765–1770

RARITY: Very rare

BORDER NOS: 69

MARKS: Usually none

SHAPES USED: Plain thrown and turned coffee cups and teabowls, perhaps with matching saucers.

COMMENTARY: It is somewhat unusual to find a pattern simply consisting of a small band or frieze to be painted around the centre of a shape, with large areas of unadorned white at the top and bottom, and it is probable that the design did not find favour with the purchasers of the day, hence its comparative rarity. A glost fragment with a very similar border to that used with this pattern was found in the excavations, but there was no evidence of the design itself. The Victoria and Albert Museum own a teabowl decorated with the pattern.

Coffee Cup, 3¼ in. high
(Gilbert Bradley Collection)

Coffee Cup
Complete pattern

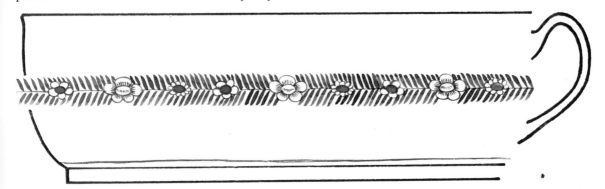

Teapot (lacking cover), 3⅞ in. high (Authors' Collections)

DATE RANGE: *c.* 1785

RARITY: Very rare

BORDER NOS: 14

MARKS: Open crescent

SHAPES USED: Plain thrown and turned teawares, including the teapot illustrated, which, with its missing cover supplied, would be about 4½ in. high.

COMMENTARY: This pattern is one of the very last blue and white floral paintings to have originated at the Worcester works, and shows clearly the highly stylized decoration which had come into common use at that time. The border used here is very similar to that found on the 'Mimosa' (Pattern I. F.9), and on 'The Birds in Branches' (II.B.21) printed patterns being made around the same time. The subsidiary sprays used here are identical to those employed on the 'Mimosa' pattern as well. A glost waster of a teapot cover decorated with this design was found in the factory site excavations, but did not fit the authors' teapot illustrated – not unusual in itself, as covers were generally made to fit a particular piece whose sizes could vary substantially from example to example.

I. The Painted Patterns

F. Formal Patterns

The Maltese Cross Flower

DATE RANGE: 1770–1780

RARITY: Not uncommon

BORDER NOS: 1

MARKS: Usually none; occasionally, open crescent.

SHAPES USED: Press-moulded spoons, either solid or pierced, $5\frac{1}{4}$ in. to $5\frac{1}{2}$ in. long.

COMMENTARY: This design, taken from a Chinese original, is easily identified by its consistent arrangement, although the actual quality of the painting can vary from the very skilful to the haphazard work that became more common toward the end of the 1770s. It is believed that this shape was only used with underglaze blue, and does not occur with polychrome decoration. These spoons are found very rarely with either 'The Gilliflower' (Pattern I.E.12) or 'The Fisherman and Cormorant' (Pattern II.A.19) designs. Biscuit fragments of spoons decorated with the pattern were found in the factory site excavations. The Godden Reference Collection owns a spoon of Lowestoft manufacture decorated with a very similar design.

Spoon, $5\frac{1}{2}$ in. long
(Dyson Perrins Museum)

Plate, 9 in. diameter
(Authors' Collections)

Mark

DATE RANGE: 1770–1780

RARITY: Not uncommon

BORDER NOS: 1

MARKS: It has its own unique mark, as illustrated.

SHAPES USED: A complete range of press-moulded dessert wares, including lobed plates, heart- or oval-shaped dishes, shell-shaped dishes, square lobed dishes, sauce tureens, covers and stands.

COMMENTARY: This design is a fairly direct copy of a K'ang Hsi original 'precious objects' decoration. Examples of the pattern can be found in a number of public porcelain collections, including those of the Victoria and Albert and Dyson Perrins Museums. Two further sizes of the lobed plate illustrated here are shown in Sandon (Plate 100) and in Spero (page 140).

The K'ang Hsi Lotus

DATE RANGE: 1770–1775

RARITY: Uncommon

BORDER NOS: None

MARKS: It has its own unique mark, as illustrated.

SHAPES USED: The pattern can be found on a wide range of both thrown and turned and press-moulded shapes, primarily dessertwares of the usual variety.

COMMENTARY: This is another of a small class of elaborate designs which appear to deliberately emulate an original K'ang Hsi design to the point of deception. The background colouration of the pattern employs a similar painting technique to that used in 'The Cracked Ice Ground' (Pattern I.A.14). Sandon illustrates an oval (or diamond-shaped) dish (Plate 101), and Hobson shows a scallop-rimmed plate (Plate XIX, top right).

Shell Dish, $11\frac{1}{2}$ in. diameter (Dyson Perrins Museum)

Mark

Saucer, $4\frac{1}{2}$ in. diameter
(Rous Lench Collection)

DATE RANGE: *c.* 1765

RARITY: Very rare

BORDER NOS: I

MARKS: Open crescent

SHAPES USED: A teabowl and saucer ($4\frac{1}{2}$ in. diameter) are known, and it was probably used on the usual range of tewares.

COMMENTARY: One should compare this design with that of 'The Arcade' (Pattern I.A.7) for the obvious relationship between the two. This rare pattern has some resemblance to an earlier Delft design which may have been its origin. Both the teabowl and the saucer illustrated are owned by a private collector, and no examples are known within the major public collections.

Bowl, 6 in. diameter
(Authors' Collections)

DATE RANGE: *c.* 1770

RARITY: Uncommon

BORDER NOS: 1

MARKS: Open crescents, script 'W' marks, or an unusual script 'W' enclosed in an oblong lozenge.

SHAPES USED: Plain thrown and turned tewares, and mugs of various sizes.

COMMENTARY: The Sèvres factory made a variety of somewhat similar coloured designs to that of the Worcester factory, and it is difficult to say whether the English version was taken from these or directly from Japanese originals upon which the Sèvres patterns were based. Worcester made the pattern in underglaze blue without the floral decoration as well, illustrated here as 'The Queen's Pattern' (I.F.6). A few biscuit fragments decorated with the design were found in the excavations at the site of the original factory. Hobson illustrates the Japanese-design bowl (Plate XXXI), probably the origin of the Worcester version, and Rissik Marshall also illustrates the English pattern (Plate 8 [138]). Examples can be found in the British Museum and in the H. R. Marshall Collection at the Ashmolean Museum, Oxford.

*Saucer, 4¾ in. diameter
(Authors' Collections)*

DATE RANGE: *c.* 1770

RARITY: Very rare

BORDER NOS: 52

MARKS: None

SHAPES USED: We have only seen a pair of saucers, as illustrated, but think it likely that the pattern was used on the normal range of teawares.

COMMENTARY: This is a very common Worcester design in gold onglaze decoration, but that is normally found either with no border or with an entirely different border from that used in the underglaze blue pattern. While undoubtedly of Worcester origin, it is nevertheless highly unusual to find the design utilized in the blue and white decoration.

The Trellis Lily

DATE RANGE: 1780–1785

RARITY: Very rare

BORDER NOS: None

MARKS: Open crescent

SHAPES USED: The pattern appears to be confined to use with teabowls and saucers, the latter of the usual $4\frac{1}{2}$ in. diameter.

COMMENTARY: This pattern is nothing more than a simpler and more stylized off-shoot of the common 'Royal Lily' design (Pattern I.F.8), and a careful examination of the two will confirm their close relationship. There are several examples of these teabowls and saucers in private collections, all of which are marked with the Worcester crescent, and all undoubtedly originating at that factory.

Teabowl, $3\frac{1}{8}$ in. diameter
(Authors' Collections)

DATE RANGE: 1775 into the 19th century

RARITY: Common

BORDER NOS: 43 in gold over a solid blue band.

MARKS: Open crescent

SHAPES USED: The pattern will be found to appear on every possible shape made at the factory, both thrown and turned, jolleyed and press-moulded shapes, including a complete range of teawares and dessert-wares, and tub-shaped tea and coffee cups, together with mugs of all sizes.

COMMENTARY: You will find that this pattern has almost invariably been embellished by either gilding or the addition of a 'rouge de fer' type rim, and it is most unusual to find an example in the unenhanced blue colour only. The design is usually carefully but boldly painted, with little discernible variation in its treatment. The pattern takes its name from an order placed with the factory by George III in 1788, when he purchased a complete service decorated with the 'Lily' design. Several other rival factories also used the pattern, including Caughley (1780), and its successor at Coalport, John Rose (c. 1800). The pattern was also made by Chamberlain's factory in Worcester in the 1795–1800 period. Like the 'Music' design (Pattern I.F.11), the 'Royal Lily' was also used in conjunction with armorial pieces, decorating all but the reserved panels. Quantities of biscuit and glost wasters of the pattern were found in the factory site excavations.

Teapot Stand, $5\frac{2}{5}$ in. diameter (Dyson Perrins Museum)

The Mimosa

Teabowl, 3⅜ in. diameter
(Authors' Collections)

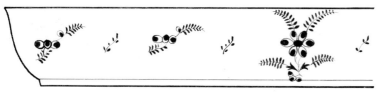

Teabowl
Complete pattern

DATE RANGE: *c.* 1780

RARITY: Very rare

BORDER NOS: 15

MARKS: Open crescent

SHAPES USED: The pattern was presumably used on the normal range of teawares, although we have only seen it with teabowls and saucers (the latter of the usual 4½ in. diameter).

COMMENTARY: The style of this design falls somewhere between 'The Trellis Lily' (Pattern I.F.7) seen earlier and the well-known 'Immortelle' (Pattern I.F.10) which follows. From the few examples known, and from the absence of evidence in the waster pits uncovered by the factory site excavations, it is probable that the pattern was not used extensively at the Worcester factory. The examples we have seen of the pattern, all in private collections, are always marked with the Worcester crescent.

Immortelle

DATE RANGE: 1765–1780

RARITY: Not uncommon

BORDER NOS: 1

MARKS: Open crescent, if any.

SHAPES USED: Press-moulded or jolleyed teawares, in the normal range.

COMMENTARY: Sometimes incorrectly referred to as 'The Meissen Onion' pattern, this design was actually most widely used by the Copenhagen and Thuringian factories. Lowestoft also made an 'Immortelle' type pattern, which Watney illustrates in Plate 80(C). The Worcester version shows an unvarying treatment, using bold, single stroke painting, but the arrangement is necessarily altered to fit the shape decorated. A number of biscuit fragments were found in the excavations, and Sandon illustrates one of these (Plate 106), alongside a completed teabowl and saucer. Similar shapes are also illustrated by Hobson (Plate XIX, top left), and by Severne Mackenna (Plate 13 [26]).

*Saucer, 5 in. diameter
(Dyson Perrins Museum)*

*Teacup
Complete pattern*

The Music

DATE RANGE: 1785 into the 19th
century

RARITY: Uncommon

BORDER NOS: 43 in gold on a
solid blue band

MARKS: Open crescent

SHAPES USED: The normal
range of plain thrown and turned
teawares, and, more rarely, press-
moulded dessertwares.

COMMENTARY: Like the 'Royal
Lily' (Pattern I.F.8), 'The Music'
design is most often found to
have been embellished by the
addition of gilding or a 'rouge de
fer' rim edge. Also in company
with that pattern, it is seen on
pieces having reserved panels
decorated with polychrome
armorials. The pattern was
continued after 1800 by Flight,
Barr and Barr at the Worcester
factory. Glost fragments with the
pattern were found in the late
levels of the factory site
excavations. Several examples of
the design can be seen at the
Dyson Perrins Museum.

*Sucrier and Cover, 5 in. high
(Authors' Collections)*

II. The Printed Patterns

A. Prominent Figures

The Tea Party

*Saucer, $4\frac{5}{8}$ in. diameter
(Dyson Perrins Museum)*

DATE RANGE: 1758–1760

RARITY: Very rare

BORDER NOS: None

MARKS: None

SHAPES USED: The only known example is the plain thrown and turned saucer illustrated, which is $4\frac{5}{8}$ in. diameter.

COMMENTARY: This is an underglaze blue version of an engraving used primarily for onglaze transfer-prints. The engraving was done by Robert Hancock about 1758, and the print illustrated is most unusual in that it appears to have been taken from the same copper plate employed in the onglaze examples, rather than being re-engraved with somewhat heavier lines as was generally done. Cyril Cook (Item 106) tells us that there were several of these 'Tea Party' engravings done by Hancock of which this example is the third. The onglaze print is signed 'R. Hancock fecit'.

*Mug, $5\frac{7}{8}$ in. high
(Authors' Collections)*

DATE RANGE: 1775–1785

RARITY: Rare

BORDER NOS: None

MARKS: Hatched crescent

SHAPES USED: A range of plain thrown and turned cylinder mugs, from $3\frac{1}{3}$ in. to $5\frac{7}{8}$ in. high.

COMMENTARY: This is the first, and most uncommon, of three related shooting scenes, the others being Patterns II.A.3 and 4 hereafter. While the engravings can probably be said to be 'in the manner of' Robert Hancock, we have never seen this design or the other 'shooting' prints used in an onglaze version, and no mention is made of them by Cook.

The Man Aiming a Gun

DATE RANGE: 1775–1785

RARITY: Uncommon

BORDER NOS: None

MARKS: Hatched crescent

SHAPES USED: A range of plain thrown and turned cylinder mugs, $3\frac{1}{3}$ in. to $5\frac{7}{8}$ in. high.

COMMENTARY: This design is usually found in conjunction with 'The Man Shooting a Gun' (Pattern II.A.4), or, more rarely, with the preceding pattern, and like its related patterns, appears to have been confined to use on cylinder mugs. As far as we know, the pattern was not used for onglaze transfer-prints. Glost fragments of the pattern were found in the excavations. Godden illustrates a similar small mug (Plate 254 [right]), and examples can be seen in several public collections, including the Victoria and Albert Museum.

Mug, $3\frac{1}{2}$ in. high
(Dyson Perrins Museum)

The Man Shooting a Gun

Mug, $5\frac{7}{8}$ in. high
(Authors' Collections)

DATE RANGE: 1775–1785

RARITY: Uncommon

BORDER NOS: None

MARKS: Hatched crescent

SHAPES USED: A range of plain thrown and turned cylinder mugs, varying in size from $3\frac{1}{3}$ in. to $5\frac{7}{8}$ in. high.

COMMENTARY: This is the last of the 'shooting' patterns trilogy, and perhaps the best known of the three. Like its related designs, it can be said to be in the manner of Hancock, although unlikely to have been engraved by him, as it does not seem to have been used on the onglaze decorated ware in the decade preceding. Godden illustrates a $4\frac{3}{4}$ in. mug with this design in his Caughley-Worcester book (Plate 254). A few glost wasters with this pattern were found in the excavations, although no biscuit fragments were located there.

Left: *Mug, 5½ in. high*
(Dyson Perrins Museum)

Right: *Mug*
Reverse pattern

DATE RANGE: 1775–1780

RARITY: Rare

BORDER NOS: None

MARKS: Hatched crescent

SHAPES USED: This pattern is found both on plain thrown and turned cylinder mugs of various sizes, as well as on a press-moulded, cabbage-leaf mask jug around 10 in. high.

COMMENTARY: This design was engraved by Robert Hancock (see Cook, Item 42), and adapted by him from a painting entitled *In Full Chase* by James Seymour. The design was used fairly extensively in onglaze printing, but from the few examples now known, its use in the underglaze blue was limited. A cabbage-leaf mask jug decorated with the design was sold by Christie's on 2 June 1969 (Lot 96), but its present ownership is unknown.

DATE RANGE: *c.* 1790

RARITY: Very rare

BORDER NOS: None

MARKS: None

SHAPES USED: A press-moulded, cabbage-leaf jug with mask spout, $9\frac{1}{2}$ in. high.

COMMENTARY: The scene illustrated was originally engraved by James Ross, and was used in onglaze printing during the 1760s, the prints usually bearing the signature of Ross. The only underglaze blue version was done much later and was unsigned. The known example is on a cabbage-leaf mask jug owned by the Masonic Lodge at Worcester. As no photograph of this jug was available, the illustration shown has been taken from a 'pull' from the original copper plate engraving still owned by the Dyson Perrins Museum, so the positions of the details are necessarily shown in reverse to those appearing on the actual shape decorated.

Copper Plate 'Pull'
(Dyson Perrins Museum)

Bowl, 5⅞ in. diameter
(Authors' Collections)

Bowl
Reverse pattern

DATE RANGE: 1775–1790

RARITY: Not uncommon

BORDER NOS: Q

MARKS: Hatched crescent or disguised numerals.

SHAPES USED: An extensive range of teawares, primarily plain thrown and turned shapes.

COMMENTARY: A version of the design, traditionally attributed to Hancock, was frequently used in onglaze printing from about 1760, and is referred to by Cook (Item 73). The engravings used for underglaze blue decoration show some variations in the components included, and were apparently done by various hands over the period of the pattern's use. In some examples, you can see either a ladder or a stile leaning against the hayrack in the background, while on others they are missing. By 1788, the Chamberlain factory in Worcester was marketing teawares decorated with this print which had been embellished by the addition of a gilt rim, advertising a complete 43-piece tea set for six shillings, a reasonable price even at the economic level of that day. A variety of both biscuit and glost wasters of the design were found in the excavations.

DATE RANGE : 1761–1765

RARITY : Very rare

BORDER NOS : None

MARKS : None

SHAPES USED : Plain thrown and turned cylinder mugs, ranging in size from $3\frac{3}{8}$ in. to $5\frac{3}{4}$ in. high.

COMMENTARY : This is the underglaze blue version of the *c.* 1760 Hancock onglaze transfer-print, with the engraved lines somewhat strengthened for use with the underglaze colour. The original Hancock plate is illustrated by Cook (Item 54). The portrait of the King is after an engraving by James McArdell from a painting by Jeremiah Mayer. The subsidiary subjects, 'Fame' and 'Britannia', are used both on this pattern and on that of 'Queen Charlotte' (Pattern II.A.9) which follows, and were probably used interchangeably, as the mugs were sold by the factory as a pair. The 'Fame' engraving is shown in Cook as the third depiction of this figure (Item 33).

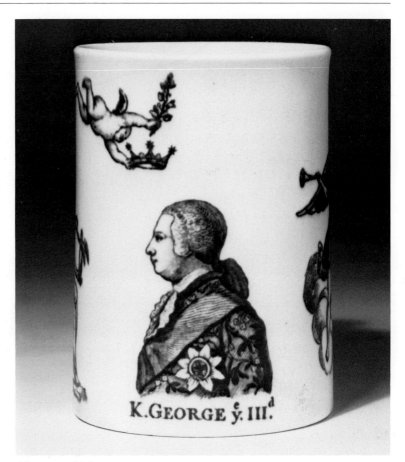

Mug, 5 in. high
(Dyson Perrins Museum)

Mug
Britannia pattern

Mug
Fame pattern

DATE RANGE: 1761–1765

RARITY: Very rare

BORDER NOS: None

MARKS: None

SHAPES USED: Plain thrown and turned cylinder mugs, ranging in size from $3\frac{3}{8}$ in. to $5\frac{3}{4}$ in. high.

COMMENTARY: Like the George III engraving preceding (Pattern II.A.8), this pattern was derived originally from an engraving by James McArdell done in 1761, the year of the coronation and marriage of George III. The onglaze print is shown in Cook (Item 91), and in Hobson (Plate XLIX, top left). The engraving of 'Minerva', which can be seen at the Queen's right side, is pictured in Cook (Item 74). As mentioned earlier, these subsidiary designs were probably used interchangeably on mugs decorated with this pattern and with the George III engraving, as the pieces were usually sold as a pair. The small mug illustrated was offered for sale in December 1979 by Hoff Antiques, the London porcelain dealers (see *The Antique Collector* for that month, page 74), with both sides of the mug being illustrated, as shown here.

Mug, $3\frac{3}{8}$ in. high
(The Antique Collector)

La Pêche/La Promenade Chinoise

▲ *Mug, 5¼ in. high*
(Dyson Perrins Museum)

▼ *Mug*
Reverse pattern

DATE RANGE: 1770–1785

RARITY: Common

BORDER NOS: None

MARKS: Hatched crescent or disguised numerals.

SHAPES USED: Plain thrown and turned cylinder, bell-shaped, and wide-bodied mugs of a variety of sizes.

COMMENTARY: The two designs of this pattern are taken from illustrations in *The Ladies' Amusement*, pages 113 and 148, the latter signed 'J. June, sculp.' The original engraving for the onglaze print was done by Hancock from these illustrations which, in turn, had been taken from an engraving in 1758 by Canot after Jean Pillement, whose work had first appeared in a book entitled *Livre de Chinoise*. See Cook, pages 81–8. Caughley did a very similar underglaze print which can only be distinguished by careful examination, as explained by Godden (pages 133–4), and illustrated by him (Plates 258B and 259B). On the very large pieces, such as the cider mug we have illustrated, the two basic designs were often supplemented with a third pattern, 'The Temple Bells' (Pattern II.B.7). Many wasters of the design, both biscuit and glost, were found in the factory site excavations.

Teabowl and Saucer, the latter 4¼ in. diameter
(Sotheby Parke Bernet and Co.)

DATE RANGE: 1770–1780

RARITY: Uncommon

BORDER NOS: I

MARKS: Hatched crescent or script 'W'

SHAPES USED: Plain thrown and turned teawares, of the normal range.

COMMENTARY: Both biscuit and glost wasters decorated with this design were found in the excavations of the original factory site. The Dyson Perrins Museum has an example of the pattern in its collection at Worcester. A similar but not identical pattern was made by the Pennington's factory at Liverpool, probably a copy of the Worcester original.

Bowl, 5⅞ in. diameter
(Authors' Collections)

DATE RANGE: 1775–1785

RARITY: Rare

BORDER NOS: 1, if any.

MARKS: Hatched crescent

SHAPES USED: Plain thrown and turned bowls, ranging in size from 5½ in. to 8 in. in diameter.

COMMENTARY: This rare design is not actually a pattern in its own right, for it is only found as the occasional reverse design of another pattern, 'The Mother and Child' (II.A.13). Godden states that it occurs in two versions, but the one illustrated is certainly the more usual of these and is the only one which we have seen. The name of the pattern is derived from an early onglaze transfer-print which is markedly different from this design. An example may be seen at the Godden Reference Collection in Worthing, and is illustrated in Godden's work on Caughley and Worcester porcelains (Plate 257).

The Mother and Child

DATE RANGE: 1775–1785

RARITY: Rare (the three-figure version) to common (with two figures)

BORDER NOS: 1, if any.

MARKS: Hatched crescent, sometimes with added letters.

SHAPES USED: Plain thrown and turned teawares, in the normal range.

COMMENTARY: There are two variations of this pattern, as illustrated, with the more common having two figures, a mother and child, and the rarer, shown on the bowl, with a second woman included. The Caughley factory did a similar but distinguishable pattern (see Godden, page 255), as did the John Rose establishment at Coalport. Both biscuit and glost fragments decorated with the design were found in the factory site excavations. Godden illustrates two further examples of the Worcester pattern (Plates 255A and 256).

▲ *Teapot and Cover, 6 in. high (Sotheby Parke Bernet and Co.)*

▼ *Bowl, 5⅞ in. diameter (Authors' Collections)*

The Man Leaning on a Fence

Left: *Mug, 3½ in. high
(Gilbert Bradley Collection)*
Right: *Mug
Reverse pattern*

DATE RANGE: *c.* 1765

RARITY: Rare

BORDER NOS: None

MARKS: None

SHAPES USED: Plain thrown and turned cylinder mugs, usually around 3½ in. high.

COMMENTARY: The reverse design of this rare print is reminiscent of that in 'The Two Swan Precipice' (Pattern II.B.3), and is undoubtedly related to it. The principal design is possibly derived from a Pillement engraving, as it is certainly in that style. There are several examples of these mugs in private collections. Sotheby's sold another in its 7 October 1969 sale (Lot 157).

Mug, 5 in. high
(Sotheby Parke Bernet and Co.)

DATE RANGE: *c.* 1775

RARITY: Very rare

BORDER NOS: None

MARKS: Hatched crescent

SHAPES USED: A plain thrown and turned cylinder mug, 5 in. high.

COMMENTARY: The only known example of this print was sold by Sotheby's as a part of the Jenkins Collection on 28 April 1970 (Lot 14), and we are unaware of its present ownership. The reverse design on the mug, of which we have no picture, depicts an Oriental playing a mandolin in front of a young boy, who is seated on a drum-like object and is waving sticks before a background pagoda. The entire design is very much in the style of Jean Pillement, and was probably taken from one of his drawings.

Les Garçons Chinois

DATE RANGE: *c.* 1760

RARITY: Rare

BORDER NOS: None

MARKS: None

SHAPES USED: Plain thrown and turned mugs, including bell-shaped mugs similar to that illustrated, about 6 in. high, and smaller cylinder mugs, usually around 4 in. high.

COMMENTARY: The underglaze transfer-print used for this pattern was accomplished by the direct use of the engraved plate intended for onglaze black or coloured-in transfer-print decoration, and as a result, the underglaze example is very frequently marred by extensive blurring. This print is usually attributed to an engraving by Robert Hancock (see Cook, Item 44) after the style of Jean Pillement. As can be seen, it shows two Oriental boys, one of whom is sawing through the scroll upon which the other is seated. As seen on the mug illustrated, one can find pieces decorated with the sawn-off scroll and seated boy placed in a different position from that shown in the 'pull' from the original engraved plate still in the possession of the Dyson Perrins Museum. The illustration shown in Cook is the more elaborate version of the pattern which, to our knowledge, was never used in the underglaze blue version. The pattern from the copper plate 'pull', of course, appears here in reverse from that which would be found on an actual example.

Mug, 6 in. high (China Choice Antiques)

Below:
Copper Plate 'Pull' (Dyson Perrins Museum)

DATE RANGE: 1775–1780

RARITY: Not uncommon

BORDER NOS: 1

MARKS: Hatched crescent or script 'W'.

SHAPES USED: Plain thrown and turned teawares.

COMMENTARY: When one considers the very elaborate frame surrounding the central cartouche of this pattern, it is surprising to find that the primary design is of figures engraved in a naïve and even crude fashion. Generally the pattern will be repeated on each side of hollow-ware pieces. A somewhat similar design was used at Penningtons in Liverpool, but should be easily distinguishable. Quantities of both biscuit and glost wasters were found in the excavations of the original Worcester factory site, one of which is illustrated by Sandon (Plate 132). Examples can be seen at several of the major public collections, including the Dyson Perrins Museum and the Victoria and Albert Museum.

Bowl, 6 in. diameter (Authors' Collections)

Bowl Interior pattern

Potted Meat Tub, 5⅛ in. long
(Private Collection)

DATE RANGE: *c.* 1760

RARITY: Very rare

BORDER NOS: None

MARKS: Hatched crescent, if any.

SHAPES USED: The pattern is known to occur on two shapes, the oval potted meat tub illustrated, and a small bell-shaped mug, 3¼ in. high.

COMMENTARY: The potted meat tub illustrated is owned by a private collector in the United States, and the bell-shaped mug is illustrated by Barrett (Plate 45), a piece from his own collection. The decoration on the exterior of the potted meat tub is 'The Early Peony Print' (Pattern II.C.4), and this may appear on the reverse of the Barrett mug as well.

Bowl, 10⅛ in. diameter
(Authors' Collections)

DATE RANGE: 1775–1790

RARITY: Common

BORDER NOS: M or, more rarely, N

MARKS: Hatched crescent or disguised numerals.

SHAPES USED: A very wide range of plain thrown and turned teawares and other shapes, as well as specialty pieces such as the large bowl illustrated.

COMMENTARY: The Caughley factory made a very similar print which usually (but not always) can be distinguished by the fat fish in the hands of the foreground figure, and the straight line on the pole of the distant fisherman, contrasting with the longer and more slender fish of the Worcester version, along with the wavy line of the distant fishing pole. The swags along the border of the bowl illustrated are not typical, and are present only on the larger hollow-ware pieces. In the records of the Chamberlain factory, the pattern is always referred to as 'Pleasure Boat', and it was frequently embellished by that factory with added gilding. As noted in chapter 1, a complete tea service in this pattern was sold by Worcester in 1788 for a total sum of five shillings and sixpence, which Chamberlain noted as being somewhat cheaper than a set in the same pattern produced at Caughley. Vast quantities of biscuit and glost fragments of the pattern were uncovered at several levels of the factory site excavations.

DATE RANGE: *c.* 1780

RARITY: Rare

BORDER NOS: 0

MARKS: Disguised numerals

SHAPES USED: Plain thrown and turned miniature teawares, including a teabowl (2 in. diameter) and saucer (3½ in. diameter).

COMMENTARY: The engraving on the teabowl, showing a nursemaid with two children, was taken from the drawing book of John Bowles, dated 23 November 1756, and was illustrated by Anthony Ray in his book, *English Delftware Tiles*, figure 55, as used on Tile No. 667. The 'Wheeling Chair' engraving is of unknown origin, but may well be from a Bowles design as well. A version of this pattern was used by Worcester in an earlier onglaze print, signed 'R. Hancock fecit' (see Cook, Item 116). Two teapots with this design are recorded, each of them with two new designs, one of which has a girl in a swing with a man standing alongside. We have not seen the other teapot. All of the known copies of this pattern are in private collections, one example of which was exhibited as Item 61 in the 1979 Albert Amor showing of 18th Century English Soft Paste Porcelains.

Miniature Teabowl and Saucer, 3½ in. diameter (Private Collection)

II. The Printed Patterns

B. Landscapes, Birds and Animals

The Man in the Pavilion

*Saucer, 4¾ in. diameter
(Authors' Collections)*

DATE RANGE: 1757–1760

RARITY: Not uncommon

BORDER NOS: Usually none

MARKS: Both printed open and hatched crescents.

SHAPES USED: Plain thrown and turned teawares.

COMMENTARY: This is one of the earliest underglaze blue transfer-printed designs. A slightly earlier black onglaze print of a similar style is known to have been made at Worcester, and may have been the source of this engraving. The pattern can vary considerably in arrangement when used on hollow-ware shapes, and must be studied carefully if it is to be properly identified. A few biscuit and glost fragments of the design were found at early levels of the excavation of the factory site. This is the first example of a style of engraving that will carry forward through the next five designs (Patterns II.B.2–6).

The Creeper Print

Saucer, 4¾ in. diameter (Gilbert Bradley Collection)

DATE RANGE: 1757–1760

RARITY: Very rare

BORDER NOS: None

MARKS: None

SHAPES USED: The pattern is only known on the 4¾ in. saucer illustrated.

COMMENTARY: The style of engraving used in this print has strong links with that of the preceding pattern and the four designs which follow, and it is entirely possible that they were all the work of a single craftsman. You will also see a close stylistic connection with the painted 'Peony Creeper' pattern (I.D.30) which appeared some years later.

Saucer, 4½ in. diameter
(Gilbert Bradley Collection)

DATE RANGE: 1757–1760

RARITY: Very rare

BORDER NOS: None

MARKS: None

SHAPES USED: We have only seen this pattern on these plain thrown and turned saucers, all about 4½ in. in diameter.

COMMENTARY: Here again we see an engraving style closely resembling that of 'The Man in the Pavilion' (Pattern II.B.1) and possibly done by the same hand. The subject matter of this design is akin to that on the reverse of 'The Man Leaning on a Fence' (Pattern II.A.14). We are aware of only three examples of this rare print, all of which are in private collections.

The Swan Boat Tureen

Tureen and Cover, 18¼ in. long (Christie, Manson and Woods Ltd)

DATE RANGE: 1757–1760

RARITY: Very rare

BORDER NOS: None

MARKS: None

SHAPES USED: A press-moulded, heavily modelled oval tureen and cover, about 18¼ in. in length, with moulded dolphin finial and modelled handles.

COMMENTARY: It is interesting to see a piece of this importance decorated with a transfer-print design, as all of the others we have noted (see 'The Tureen Panel Group', Pattern I.A.11) have been hand-painted. This possibly reflects the attitude of the Worcester factory owners towards transfer-printing as being of equal importance and desirability as a decoration, at least during this period. The tureen illustrated was sold by Christie's on 21 April 1969 (Lot 72) and was used by Watney as Colour Plate B (facing page 42) of his book. The design is, again, a continuation of the engraving style first seen in Pattern II.B.1.

DATE RANGE: 1760–1770

RARITY: Not uncommon

BORDER NOS: Usually none; rarely 63 on teawares.

MARKS: Hatched crescent, if any.

SHAPES USED: Both plain thrown and turned as well as press-moulded shapes, including a complete range of teawares, mugs of various sizes and shapes, octagonal saucers, hexagonal teapot stands, etc.

COMMENTARY: This printed design is an almost exact copy of the painted 'Plantation' (Pattern I.D.11), whose name is given to this transfer-print. The engraving used here is stylistically similar to that employed in 'The Man in the Pavilion' (Pattern II.B.1), but forms the link with the more common 'Fence' (Pattern II.B.9) that eventually replaces it after about 1770. The factory site excavations produced fragments in both biscuit and glost which were decorated with this design. Examples of the pattern can be seen at most public exhibitions of Worcester porcelains, including the Victoria and Albert and Dyson Perrins Museums.

Left: *Mug, 6 in. high (Authors' Collections)*
Right: *Mug Reverse pattern*

The Bamboo Billboards

Leaf Tray, 3¼ in. long
(Godden Reference Collection)

DATE RANGE: 1757–1760

RARITY: Very rare

BORDER NOS: 4

MARKS: None

SHAPES USED: A press-moulded leaf tray, 3¼ in. long.

COMMENTARY: This is the last of six early prints linked primarily through their style of engraving, beginning with 'The Man in the Pavilion' (Pattern II.B.1). The example illustrated is the only one known to us. A biscuit waster decorated with the pattern was found in the factory site excavations.

*Mug, $5\frac{1}{3}$ in. high
(Dyson Perrins Museum)*

DATE RANGE: *c.* 1775

RARITY: Very rare

BORDER NOS: None

MARKS: Hatched crescent

SHAPES USED: This design appears only on large thrown and turned shapes, including the wide mug illustrated, which was probably intended for use as a cider mug. It is also found on a large punchbowl, around 14 in. in diameter.

COMMENTARY: As far as we can tell, this pattern is used exclusively as a subsidiary design to supplement a primary decoration on very large shapes. The mug illustrated is decorated on two sides with the 'La Pêche/ La Promenade Chinoise' prints (Pattern II.A.10), with this design used as the third pattern. On the punchbowl mentioned, it is used in conjunction with 'The Argument' (Pattern II.B.10) as a space filler.

The Wellhouse

▲ *Creamboat, $3\frac{1}{2}$ in. high*
(Authors' Collections)

▼ *Creamboat*
Reverse pattern

DATE RANGE: *c.* 1785

RARITY: Very rare

BORDER NOS: Q

MARKS: Hatched crescent

SHAPES USED: A press-moulded, 'Chelsea ewer'-type creamboat, $3\frac{1}{2}$ in. high.

COMMENTARY: Like the previous 'Temple Bells' (Pattern II.B.7), this engraving is very much in the style of the Anglo-French artist Jean Pillement, and was probably derived from one of his drawings. Note that the border used here is the same as that employed on the more common 'Milkmaids' (Pattern II.A.7). Another example of this pattern is owned by the Godden Reference Collection in Worthing.

Chocolate Cup Stand, 5¾ in. diameter (Authors' Collections)

DATE RANGE: 1765–1785

RARITY: Common

BORDER NOS: 2, F, or more rarely, 76

MARKS: Printed open and hatched crescents, the latter sometimes with added letters, or rarely, the 'Man in the Moon'.

SHAPES USED: A comprehensive range of thrown and turned shapes, as well as a few press-moulded pieces, including the normal range of teawares, miniature teawares, chocolate (or caudle) cups and stands, mustard pots, spittoons, etc.

COMMENTARY: This was surely the most popular of all of the Worcester underglaze blue printed designs, and was necessarily adapted to fit the wide range of shapes on which it was used. As a result there can be some considerable variation in the arrangement of the components of the pattern, and is even found with the two birds above the lake flying in an opposite direction from those on the chocolate cup stand illustrated. Several of Worcester's competitors were quick to copy the pattern, and similar versions can be found in Caughley (see Godden, Plate 262A), Lowestoft (see Watney, Plate 85C), and Derby (Watney, Plate 67C), although each of these can be distinguished by careful comparison. Quantities of biscuit and glost fragments were found at every level of the excavations corresponding to the date range of this pattern.

DATE RANGE: 1775–1785, possibly later

RARITY: Not uncommon

BORDER NOS: S

MARKS: Disguised numerals and, rarely, hatched crescents.

SHAPES USED: Both plain thrown and turned shapes as well as press-moulded pieces, including a normal range of teawares, mugs, tea canisters, hexagonal teapot stands, and a large, 14 in. diameter punchbowl.

COMMENTARY: This is a very complex design, and it is not surprising therefore to find considerable differences in the way in which it was used to fit the variety of shapes which it decorated. Indeed, on some of the smaller pieces, such as teabowls, it is not unusual to find that the two men in dispute in the background window have been eliminated altogether, making positive identification of the pattern all the more difficult. As with many designs of the 1780s, it can often be found with gilt embellishment. In this pattern, unlike that following (Pattern II.B.11) and others of the heavy Oriental style, the shading is done through line engraving and tight cross-hatching, often resulting in extensive blurring, and it is not easy to find an example which shows the entire pattern clearly. Both biscuit and glost fragments were found in the factory site excavations in the levels indicated by the date range. Lowestoft imitated the Worcester 'Argument' design. Godden notes this (*Lowestoft Porcelain*, page 21), but does not illustrate their version of the pattern.

Saucer Dish, $7\frac{1}{4}$ in. diameter (Authors' Collections)

*Teapot and Cover, 6 in. high
(Authors' Collections)*

DATE RANGE: 1780–1790

RARITY: Not uncommon

BORDER NOS: G

MARKS: Disguised numerals

SHAPES USED: Both plain and thrown shapes as well as jolleyed, semi-fluted shapes, as the sucrier illustrated, in the normal range of teawares.

COMMENTARY: This pattern is one of three transfer-printed designs which have been augmented by the addition of lightly shaded, washed in colours done by hand to complete the decoration and there is considerable variation in the way this has been done. It is frequently found also with gilt embellishment. The Caughley factory produced a similar pattern featuring two figures within a 'spotlight' of undecorated area, and it is very possible that Worcester used this Caughley design as its inspiration for the pattern, particularly since the Worcester version often appears on the semi-fluted shapes so frequently produced by Caughley in this period. Note that this

design is quite different in every
way from the transfer-print done
by Caughley which is now known
as 'The Temple' pattern. The
Worcester copy of this Caughley
'Temple' print was hand-painted
and is listed here as 'The
Caughley Temple' (Pattern
I.B.39). A much simplified
version of this pattern can be
found as the centre design in
moulded teawares. Several glost
fragments decorated with the
pattern were found in the factory
site excavations.

Sucrier and Cover, 6 in. high
Reverse pattern
(Authors' Collections)

The Bandstand

Coffee Pot and Cover, 8 in. high
(Dyson Perrins Museum)

DATE RANGE: 1780–1790, possibly later

RARITY: Not uncommon

BORDER NOS: I

MARKS: Hatched crescent or disguised numerals

SHAPES USED: Plain thrown and turned tewares of the normal range, and, more rarely, press-moulded shapes, including a 'gadroon'-type cream boat.

COMMENTARY: Along with two other transfer-printed patterns, 'The Worcester Temple' and 'The Bat' (II.B.11 and 26), this design is found with the addition of hand-washed blue colour augmenting the line engraved design. Some of the later pieces have also been further decorated with gilding. You may find considerable variation between the pattern as used on the smaller shapes and flatware and as used on hollow-ware. There is some dispute as to whether this pattern originated at Worcester or was actually a rough adaptation of the Caughley 'Bandstand' print which may have appeared some years earlier. Godden illustrates the Caughley version (page 22).

The Obelisk Fisherman

DATE RANGE: *c.* 1780

RARITY: Very rare

BORDER NOS: Border inside lip not illustrated.

MARKS: Disguised numerals

SHAPES USED: A press-moulded, 'gadroon' type creamboat or small sauceboat, about 4 in. long.

COMMENTARY: The only example of this rare pattern known to us is the creamboat illustrated, which is owned by Geoffrey Godden of Worthing, and pictured in his comprehensive book on Caughley and Worcester porcelains (Plate 270A).

Creamboat, 4 in. long
(Godden of Worthing Ltd)

The Obelisk and Vase

Cream Jug, 4 in. high
(Godden Reference Collection)

DATE RANGE: *c.* 1780

RARITY: Very rare

BORDER NOS: G

MARKS: Hatched crescent

SHAPES USED: A plain thrown and turned cream jug, 4 in. high.

COMMENTARY: The only known example of this pattern is the cream jug illustrated. The very detailed engraving is very much in the style of those derived from Hancock's works, as in the case of the 'Classical Ruins' group of transfer-printed patterns (II.B.19 and 20). The reverse design is Pattern II.B.16, 'The European Landscape Group', specifically the version which appears on the saucer illustrated overleaf.

DATE RANGE: 1780–1790

RARITY: Uncommon

BORDER NOS: T and U

MARKS: Hatched crescent or disguised numerals.

SHAPES USED: Plain thrown and turned tewares of the usual range.

COMMENTARY: On the hollow-ware pieces such as teabowls or jugs there are usually two scenes, the one illustrated, and another bridge design on the reverse, shown by Godden (Plate 249). Flatware usually will have only the scene illustrated on the saucer. Chamberlain's records refer to a pattern called 'Circl'd Landscape', probably this particular design. Biscuit fragments were found in the excavations at the original factory site. Godden also illustrates a teabowl of the design (Plate 235), and further examples can be seen at the Godden Reference Collection and the Victoria and Albert Museum. Geoffrey Godden has shown us a porcelain saucer, whose maker cannot be identified from available evidence, upon which a very similar design has been used. This copy can best be distinguished by the border circling the central landscape, which is different from that used on the Worcester original, but some care is merited in examining pieces decorated with this pattern.

Saucer, $4\frac{7}{8}$ in. diameter (Authors' Collections)

◄ Bowl, 5⅝ in. diameter
(Dyson Perrins Museum)

Bowl, 4¼ in. diameter
(Authors' Collections)

Coffee Cups, 2½ in. high
(Gilbert Bradley Collection)

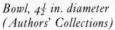

◄ Teabowl and Saucer, 5 in. diameter
(Godden of Worthing Ltd)

DATE RANGE: 1775–1785

RARITY: Uncommon

BORDER NOS: 1, if any, but M occasionally found.

MARKS: Hatched crescent or disguised numerals.

SHAPES USED: Plain thrown and turned teawares as well as small cylinder mugs.

COMMENTARY: These designs, unlike those examined previously, comprise several quite distinct subjects linked only by the common factor that each represents a country scene in a European, rather than an Oriental, setting. They are all engraved in a stylistically consistent manner, and probably by the same hand. While the examples illustrated are the only ones known to us, there could well be other variations. Note from the comparison of the two cups decorated with the windmill scene how the same design can look significantly different when represented in a differing size, even on the same shapes. Both biscuit and glost wasters were uncovered by the factory excavations, and completed examples can be found at both the Victoria and Albert and Dyson Perrins Museums. Sandon illustrates one of the excavation wasters of the pattern (Plate 137 [left]) and Godden pictures the small mug and other examples (Plates 248 [left] and 250).

*Saucer, $4\frac{7}{8}$ in. diameter
(Authors' Collections)*

DATE RANGE: 1780–1785

RARITY: Rare

BORDER NOS: G

MARKS: Hatched crescent

SHAPES USED: Jolleyed, fluted teawares, possibly of a limited range.

COMMENTARY: We have seen very few of the shapes decorated with this pattern, so are unable to state whether it is to be found on anything other than teabowls and saucers. The Dyson Perrins Museum does have one example of the pattern, similar to that illustrated. The same landscape appears on the inside bottom of the teabowl accompanying the saucer. This is a continuation of the European group of landscapes first seen in Pattern II.B.13, and exhibits the same style and content of engraving as its predecessors.

The Patty Pan Landscape

*Patty Pan, 4½ in. diameter
(Godden of Worthing Ltd)*

DATE RANGE: *c.* 1780

RARITY: Very rare

BORDER NOS: L

MARKS: Hatched crescent, if any.

SHAPES USED: A plain patty pan, 4½ in. diameter.

COMMENTARY: This rare patty pan was formerly owned by Godden of Worthing Ltd, and its present whereabouts are not known. It is the only pattern in the European landscape category to include floral sprays as a subsidiary decoration rather than the somewhat elaborate border design usually employed. The border here is unique to this design.

Bowl, 5¾ in. diameter
(Godden Reference Collection)

Teabowl, 3⅛ in. diameter
(Authors' Collections)

Teabowl
Reverse pattern

Saucer, 4⅞ in. diameter
(Authors' Collections)

DATE RANGE: 1775–1785

RARITY: Uncommon

BORDER NOS: P

MARKS: Disguised numerals

SHAPES USED: Plain thrown and turned teawares of the normal range.

COMMENTARY: This is again a group of quite distinct designs, four of which are illustrated here, and all of which feature the theme of European classical ruins and figures. Their origin dates back to Robert Hancock's onglaze transfer-print engravings of the 1760 period, but these particular underglaze blue designs did not appear until some fifteen years thereafter. The classical ruin designs used on teawares are quite different from the transfer-prints on the 'Classical Ruins Dessertwares Group' (Pattern II.B.20), as can be seen by a careful examination. Biscuit wasters decorated with the pattern were found in the factory site excavations. For further examples of the patterns illustrated here, see Sandon (Plate 138) and Godden (Plates 246, 247 and 250).

Oval Dish, $10\frac{3}{5}$ in. long
(Godden Reference Collection)

DATE RANGE: *c.* 1780

RARITY: Very rare

BORDER NOS: H and C

MARKS: Disguised numerals

SHAPES USED: We believe that, in addition to the shapes illustrated here, the pattern was also likely to have been used on other pieces of the normal dessertware service, including shell-shaped and heart-shaped dishes as well as on tureens.

COMMENTARY: Because of the rarity of this pattern, we have not been able to determine with any precision exactly how many of these classical ruin designs were actually made. We believe it was likely that the pattern was used on other shapes normally included in a dessertware service, and these could well be decorated with designs different from those shown here. This group of designs had its origin in somewhat similar onglaze black transfer-print engravings, although these had distinguishable centre designs and somewhat different border patterns as well. The round plate shown is the only example of the design owned by the Dyson Perrins Museum, and the other dishes are in the Godden Reference Collection in Worthing. Godden illustrates the oval dish in his Caughley-Worcester book (Plate 251), and uses the square dish as a colour photograph in his British Porcelain guide (see Bibliography).

*Plate, 9 in. diameter
(Dyson Perrins Museum)*

*Square Dish, $9\frac{1}{2}$ in. diameter
(Godden Reference Collection)*

307

Saucer, 5¼ in. diameter
(Dyson Perrins Museum)

Bowl, 5½ in. diameter
(Authors' Collections)

DATE RANGE: 1770–1785

RARITY: Common

BORDER NOS: Usually none, but 14 found occasionally.

MARKS: Hatched crescent

SHAPES USED: The usual range of jolleyed and thrown and turned teawares, together with some press-moulded shapes, including mask jugs of various sizes.

COMMENTARY: The pattern is traditionally credited to a Hancock printed design, and the style of the engraving suggests that this is probably so. The bowl illustrated is the usual design, and the saucer a more elaborate version of the same basic pattern, with a bird in flight as well as a third smaller bird perched on the branches below. On rounded shapes, you may find a further decoration which is a printed copy of the James Rogers-type painting of 'The Mobbing Birds' (Pattern I.C.26), and it cannot be ruled out as a possibility that the main subject was also derived from an earlier painted design. A very similar print was used by Caughley (see Godden, Plates III and 39) as well as Caughley-Coalport thereafter, and the Pennington factory at Liverpool also made a related design. The excavations in the area occupied by the original factory disclosed large quantities of both biscuit and glost fragments decorated with the pattern, and completed examples can be seen in many of the major public collections.

The Parrot Pecking Fruit / First Version

DATE RANGE: *c.* 1760

RARITY: Very rare

BORDER NOS: None

MARKS: Unknown

SHAPES USED: A plain thrown and turned cylinder mug, about 6 in. high.

COMMENTARY: The only example of this very rare 'pecking parrot' design known was in the Jenkins Collection which was sold at Sotheby's in 1970, and no picture of it appeared in the sale catalogue. As its present ownership is not known to us, we have illustrated the pattern by using an onglaze black transfer-print of the design. Comparing this mug with a picture of the Jenkins Collection mug in an article by Geoffrey Wills some years ago (*The Connoisseur*, December 1954), it is clear that the onglaze engraving was used, virtually unaltered, for the underglaze blue version as well. This pattern appeared in *The Ladies' Amusement* and was signed by Hancock, as was the black onglaze transfer-print. Cook illustrates the design (Item 78). The link with the common second version of the 'pecking parrot' design is quite obvious.

Mug, 5¼ in. high
(Dyson Perrins Museum)

DATE RANGE: 1770–1785

RARITY: Common

BORDER NOS: None

MARKS: Usually found with either the hatched crescent or a script 'W' but examples are known with a printed open crescent.

SHAPES USED: The design is usually found on plain thrown and turned shapes, primarily cylinder and bell-shaped mugs of various sizes, bottles and large jugs, but is more rarely seen on press-moulded, cabbage-leaf mask jugs as well.

COMMENTARY: As indicated in the pattern preceding (II.B.22), this decoration originated in a much simpler Hancock engraving intended for use in onglaze printing, and was illustrated originally in *The Ladies' Amusement*. There was also an intermediate onglaze print, not used in the underglaze blue, which showed fruit on a table

Mug, $5\frac{1}{4}$ in. high
(*Authors' Collections*)

Mug
Reverse pattern

with a parrot above. In addition to the sprays of currants found on the vase illustrated, you may also find a similar spray of gooseberries on some of the larger shapes, along with a beetle-like insect. Godden points out that the almost identical Caughley print of this design (which he illustrates in his book, Plates 276–80) can only be distinguished by the Worcester 'shading' which is done by cross-hatched lines rather than the straight lines used at Caughley. This is a useful rule of thumb, although, unfortunately, one can infrequently find examples where this is not so. Godden illustrates the unusual press-moulded mask jug (Plate 260), and other examples can be found in most of the major public collections of English porcelains of this period. Only a few biscuit wasters of the pattern were found in the excavations, despite the relative popularity of the design. The underglaze plate used for this design was also used for onglaze black transfer-printed decorations, but examples of these onglaze wares are extremely rare.

Vase, 8 in. high
Third pattern
(Godden Reference Collection)

*Shell Dish, 5 in. diameter
(Authors' Collections)*

DATE RANGE: *c.* 1775

RARITY: Rare

BORDER NOS: 4

MARKS: Hatched crescent

SHAPES USED: A press-moulded, scallop-shell-shaped dish, probably for use with sweetmeats, about 5 in. long, with shell-shaped handle.

COMMENTARY: Although this arguably is not a landscape, we have placed it here because of its strong stylistic link with the pattern preceding (II.B.23). The engraving style used here is much in the manner of Hancock, although we can find no engraving definitely attributed to him involving this subject matter. As far as we know, the pattern was used only on this one shape, and was not found on any of the other specialty shapes that one might expect. Godden illustrates the pattern (Plate 294), and, while we have seen several of these dishes in private collections, we do not know of any examples in major public collections.

*Plate, 7 in. diameter
(Dyson Perrins Museum)*

DATE RANGE: 1765–1770

RARITY: Very rare

BORDER NOS: I

MARKS: None

SHAPES USED: A press-moulded plate, 7 in. diameter, with basketweave rim.

COMMENTARY: This pattern was first seen as a Hancock engraving, and signed by him. It appeared in *The Ladies' Amusement* in its signed form (page 74), and was used at Worcester for onglaze black transfer-printing. Cook illustrates the design (Item 13). The pattern was later copied by the Liverpool factories, but these rather poor reproductions are easily distinguishable from the Worcester underglaze blue version. The only example of the design which we have seen is the plate illustrated here.

Dish, $10\frac{3}{8}$ in. long
(Dyson Perrins Museum)

DATE RANGE: 1780–1785

RARITY: Not uncommon

BORDER NOS: R

MARKS: Disguised numerals

SHAPES USED: The design was used on the normal range of plain thrown and turned teawares as well as on some unusual press-moulded shapes, including a tea canister with a unique border on its cover (Border Pattern E), an egg drainer, plates and scallop-edged oval dishes such as that illustrated.

COMMENTARY: For many years, this pattern was believed to have been manufactured by the Caughley factory, but is now accepted as being of solely Worcester origin. In common with 'The Worcester Temple' and 'The Bandstand' (Patterns II.B.11 and 12), it is distinguished by the addition of hand-washed colouration, and is sometimes found with gilding picking out the features of the design and its border. Many biscuit and glost fragments were found in the excavations at the factory site, and examples of complete pieces have been illustrated by several authorities, including Sandon (Plates 139, right, and 140, left), Spero (page 159) and Godden (Plates 236, 238, 239, 240, and 267). The Victoria and Albert Museum have a complete tea service decorated with the pattern.

II. The Printed Patterns

C. Floral and Fruit

The Early Creamboat Sprays

DATE RANGE: 1757–1760

RARITY: Very rare (butterboat), to not uncommon (creamboat)

BORDER NOS: None

MARKS: Hatched crescent, if any.

SHAPES USED: Press-moulded hexagonal creamboats, about $3\frac{1}{2}$ in. long, and press-moulded butterboats, $3\frac{1}{8}$ in. long.

COMMENTARY: These very simple floral sprays are among the first used at Worcester for transfer-printing. The printing is so very fine on these examples that one must look most carefully to assure oneself that they are not, in fact, painted. The pattern occurs on two rather different shapes, but both use identical sprays along their borders, and the style of design is very closely linked to one another. This is the only instance where we have knowingly departed from our system of pattern classification, ignoring the small bird on the butterboat because we felt that the link in the floral patterns was too close to separate the two designs. As noted, the butterboat is very rare, while the creamboat can be seen in several collections.

Creamboat, $3\frac{1}{2}$ in. long
(Dyson Perrins Museum)

Creamboat
Reverse pattern

Creamboat
Interior pattern

Butterboat, $3\frac{1}{8}$ in.
(Godden Reference Collection)

The Early Flowering Plants

DATE RANGE: 1758–1765

RARITY: Not uncommon

BORDER NOS: Usually none, rarely 33

MARKS: Hatched crescent, if any.

SHAPES USED: A variety of thrown and turned shapes, including teabowls (and, presumably, saucers), patty pans, and a barrel-shaped cream jug, all as illustrated.

COMMENTARY: This pattern continues the primitive style of engraving seen on the previous design, but features flowers growing from a stalk, as a complete plant rather than as separated sprays. Examples can be found in a number of private collections. The barrel jug illustrated was sold by Sotheby's on 28 April 1970 (Lot 135), as part of the Jenkins Collection. Watney illustrates this same jug (Plate 34C [left]).

Teabowl, 2¾ in. diameter
(Gilbert Bradley Collection)

Teabowl
Reverse pattern

Cream Jug, 3¼ in. high
(Sotheby Parke Bernet and Co.)

Patty Pan, 4⅛ in. diameter
(Authors' Collections)

The Spittoon Sprays

Left:
*Spittoon Rim, 5 in. diameter
(Authors' Collections)*

Right:
*Spittoon Rim, 5 in. diameter)
(Authors' Collections)*

DATE RANGE: 1765–1780

RARITY: Uncommon

BORDER NOS: None

MARKS: Hatched crescent

SHAPES USED: Plain thrown and turned spittoons, usually around 4 in. high, with 5 in. to $5\frac{1}{4}$ in. rims, with and without handles.

COMMENTARY: These sprays are found on the rims of spittoons, the bodies of which have been decorated with other transfer-printed designs. Where the larger sprays have been used on the upper rim (the spittoon on the left), you can sometimes find the smaller sprays (as on the spittoon on the right) decorating the underside of the rim.

DATE RANGE: 1758–1760

RARITY: Very rare

BORDER NOS: None

MARKS: Hatched crescent

SHAPES USED: We have seen this pattern on two shapes, a potted meat tub, $5\frac{1}{8}$ in. long, which is a press-moulded piece, and a thrown and turned, barrel-shaped, cream jug, $2\frac{3}{8}$ in. high.

COMMENTARY: While this pattern is closely related to the three previous designs, it also bears close resemblance to two painted patterns, 'Mansfield' and 'The Scalloped Peony' (I.E.1 and 9). The interior of the potted meat tub is decorated with 'The Floral Gift' (Pattern II.A.18). Both the pieces illustrated are in private collections, the tub in the United States, and the barrel jug in the west of England.

Potted Meat Tub, $5\frac{1}{8}$ in. long (Private Collection)

Cream Jug, $2\frac{3}{8}$ in. high (Private Collection)

The Rose and Running Border

DATE RANGE: 1760–1765

RARITY: Rare

BORDER NOS: None

MARKS: Printed open crescent on earliest pieces, hatched crescent thereafter.

SHAPES USED: A press-moulded butterboat with modelled exterior, 3½ in. long, and a press-moulded Blind Earl plate, 7¾ in. diameter.

COMMENTARY: It is likely that this pattern was derived from the painted 'Rose and Floral Sprays' (Pattern I.E.30). Sandon illustrates the exterior of the butterboat (Plate 111), along with a waster of the shape. The plate was sold at Sotheby's on 28 April 1970, again a part of the Jenkins Collection. The Victoria and Albert Museum have examples of the butterboat in their collection.

▲ *Blind Earl Plate, 7¾ in. diameter (Sotheby Parke Bernet and Co.)*

◄ *Butterboat, 3½ in. long (Dyson Perrins Museum)*

*Teapot and Cover, 5 in. high
(Authors' Collections)*

DATE RANGE: *c.* 1775

RARITY: Very rare

BORDER NOS: F and J

MARKS: Hatched crescent

SHAPES USED: A plain thrown and turned teapot and cover, 5 in. high.

COMMENTARY: Caughley did a version of the sprays in this pattern, using a painted border, rather than the printed ones used at Worcester. The Caughley design is equally as rare as that of Worcester. The pattern is linked to the style of both 'The Early Flowering Plants' and 'The Early Peony Print' (Patterns II.C.2 and 4), but of an obviously later date. The spout on the teapot illustrated, which is the only example of the pattern of which we are aware, has been restored to what we believe was its original shape and size.

The Natural Sprays Group

DATE RANGE: 1760–1770

RARITY: Common

BORDER NOS: 113 on junket dish

MARKS: Hatched crescent

SHAPES USED: A variety of thrown and turned, press-moulded and jolleyed shapes other than teawares, and including cylinder and bell-shaped mugs, vases, mask jugs of various sizes, junket dishes, hooped dishes, etc.

COMMENTARY: This pattern is comprised of two main naturalistic sprays, as on the two mugs shown, and usually found as primary and reverse patterns on the same piece, plus subsidiary sprays which link these to the other sprays in the group, such as those found on the mask jug illustrated. Note that on the junket dish, there is a simplified version of the main spray on the bell-shaped mug. Biscuit fragments of several of the sprays in this group were found on various waster shapes during the excavation. Lowestoft used the pattern as well, obviously copied from the Worcester original.

Junket Dish, 9 in. diameter
(Godden Reference Collection)

Mug, 6 in. high
(Dyson Perrins Museum)

Mug, 5 in. high
(Dyson Perrins Museum)

Hooped Dish, 12 in. long
(Godden of Worthing Ltd)

Jug, 10 in. high
(Dyson Perrins Museum)

Jug, 8 in high
(Dyson Perrins Museum)

Left: *Jug, 9 in. high*
(Authors' Collections)

Right: *Jug*
Reverse pattern

DATE RANGE: *c.* 1765

RARITY: Rare

BORDER NOS: Usually none, but sometimes a version of 4.

MARKS: Hatched crescent, if any.

SHAPES USED: We have seen this pattern on two press-moulded shapes, the 9 in. jug illustrated, and a shell-shaped sweetmeat dish, 5 in. long.

COMMENTARY: The pattern is made up of three main subjects, and takes its name from the flower found on the primary (right) side of the jug illustrated. The only one of the three which we have found on another shape is the rose print (reverse of the jug) which is on the shell-shaped dish mentioned. This pattern shows an effort on the part of the engraver to achieve a botanical accuracy, and possibly derives from a published botanical illustration. The subsidiary sprays here are related to those of the previous 'Natural Sprays' design (Pattern II.C.7). The jug illustrated was purchased at Phillips's sale of 26 March 1980 (Lot 189), and the shell dish is in the Godden Reference Collection.

Jug
Third pattern

DATE RANGE: 1765–1770

RARITY: Not uncommon

BORDER NOS: 76 or 33

MARKS: Hatched crescent

SHAPES USED: A variety of wares including various sized tureens and covers, press-moulded leaf trays, and plain thrown and turned spittoons.

COMMENTARY: The pattern depicts finely engraved naturalistic garden flowers of four main subjects as illustrated, with several subsidiary sprays. Occasionally, you will find the main sprays used in simplified, truncated form, but usually they will be seen as shown in the photographs. Insects will also be used on some pieces as additional decorations. A further illustration of the tureen and cover with the most unusual 'resting cow' knop can be found in Sandon (Plate 49).

Tureen and Cover, 8 in. diameter
(Dyson Perrins Museum)

Tureen Cover, 11 in. long
(Dyson Perrins Museum)

Tureen and Cover, 6½ in. long
(Dyson Perrins Museum)

Tureen and Cover
Reverse pattern

Tureen Stand, 11 in. long
(Dyson Perrins Museum)

DATE RANGE: 1765–1775

RARITY: Common

BORDER NOS: 32, 33, 35 and F.

MARKS: Hatched crescent

SHAPES USED: A variety of both press-moulded and thrown and turned shapes, including a $7\frac{1}{2}$ in. chamberpot, a buttertub, cover and stand, teapots and covers, a range of baluster-type vases, spittoons, and tureens and stands.

COMMENTARY: The pattern comprises two main sprays, as illustrated on the tureen stand and vase, with two smaller running sprays used in the border panels and on smaller pieces, together with a variety of floral sprigs. On the larger pieces, the pattern is sometimes found in conjunction with 'The Pine Cone Group' designs. The smaller sprays are very closely related to those of the 'Three Flowers' (see Patterns II.C.11 and 19). Both Caughley and Lowestoft used this design in printed patterns. Godden illustrates an oval butter tub and stand (Plate 265), and several other examples can be seen at the Dyson Perrins Museum.

Vase, 12 in. high
(Dyson Perrins Museum)

The Pine Cone Group

DATE RANGE: 1770–1785

RARITY: Not uncommon to common

BORDER NOS: 1, 32, 35, 76 (unique to the pattern) and F.

MARKS: Printed open crescent (rare), hatched crescent or script 'W'.

SHAPES USED: A very large range of both thrown and turned, jolleyed, and press-moulded shapes (other than teaware), including scallop-edged plates, pierced dishes, pierced baskets, gugglets and bottles, junket bowls, oval dishes, octagonal dishes, vases, and the range of dessert and dinner wares.

COMMENTARY: This is surely the most popular group of floral designs ever made at the Worcester factory, surpassing even the 'Three Flowers' (Pattern II.C.19) in use. Not only was it manufactured in great quantity during the eighteenth century, but it has been revived by the Worcester company on several occasions and is still sold today as 'The Rhapsody' pattern. As might be expected, volumes of both biscuit and glost wasters were found in the factory excavations at every level corresponding to its date range. The designs shown on the mask jug and the bough pot illustrated are less commonly seen than the 'Pine Cone' and its usual reverse design, 'The Ripe Pomegranate', but clearly fall into this group along with the subsidiary sprays used with them, these consisting of fruit and flowers hanging from a ribbon. A very close version of the pattern was used by both Caughley and Lowestoft.

Jug, 11 in. high
(Phillips)

Basket, 8¼ in. diameter
(Authors' Collections)

Bough Pot, 8¾ in. wide
(Godden Reference Collection)

Spittoon, 5 in. high
(Authors' Collections)

The Cabbage Rose Sprays

DATE RANGE: 1765–1770

RARITY: Not uncommon

BORDER NOS: None

MARKS: Hatched crescent

SHAPES USED: Both thrown and turned cylinder and bell-shaped mugs of various sizes and mask jugs, as illustrated, together with press-moulded, cabbage-leaf mask jugs of the normal range of sizes.

COMMENTARY: Most examples have these two sprays used front and back, as illustrated, and are linked to the 'Natural Sprays' group (Pattern II.C.7) through the subsidiary sprigs common to both. On the larger mask jugs, you can find a third spray as well, very similar in style to those illustrated, but not shown here.

Jug, 8½ in. high
(Dyson Perrins Museum)

Mug, 4½ in. high
(Godden of Worthing Ltd)

The Thorny Rose

Mug, 4½ in. high
(Dyson Perrins Museum)

DATE RANGE: 1765–1780

RARITY: Not uncommon

BORDER NOS: None

MARKS: Hatched crescent or script 'W'.

SHAPES USED: Plain thrown and turned shapes, including mugs of various sizes and punchpots (around 10 in. high), along with large press-moulded, cabbage-leaf mask jugs, 11 in. high.

COMMENTARY: This design is distinguished by the large rose print which features prominent thorns along its stem. It is sometimes found with the small subsidiary sprays from the 'Pine Cone Group' (Pattern II.C.11), and, on the mask jug, with two further large floral prints in the same style as the principal one. Caughley also made this pattern, and examples can be seen in Godden (Plates 45 and 135).

Bough Pot, 8¾ in. wide
(Christie, Manson and Woods Ltd)

Vase, 5½ in. high
(Sotheby, Parke Bernet and Co.)

DATE RANGE: 1765–1770, possibly later

RARITY: Not uncommon

BORDER NOS: None

MARKS: Hatched crescent, if any.

SHAPES USED: Both plain thrown and turned shapes such as spill vases and wine funnels, and press-moulded shapes like the bough pots illustrated.

COMMENTARY: This is really a composite group which is linked by its common use of a rose-centred motif and by the subsidiary sprays found on all of the shapes within the grouping.

Bough Pot, 8½ in. wide
(Dyson Perrins Museum)

The Wispy Chrysanthemum Sprays

Leaf Dish, 9 in. long
(Dyson Perrins Museum)

DATE RANGE: *c.* 1770

RARITY: Uncommon

BORDER NOS: None

MARKS: Hatched crescent, if any.

SHAPES USED: A press-moulded,
overlapping cabbage-leaf dish
with stock handles, 9 in. long.

COMMENTARY: The pattern
consists of a spray group of clear
arrangement and usually is found
to be well printed. It is apparently
confined to this one shape. While
no evidence was found of the
pattern itself in the various
factory site excavations, the shape
of the dish on which it appears is
well known at Worcester.

Left: *Vase, 8½ in high*
(Dyson Perrins Museum)

Right: *Vase*
Reverse pattern

DATE RANGE: 1770–1775

RARITY: Uncommon

BORDER NOS: None

MARKS: Hatched crescent, if any.

SHAPES USED: A thrown and turned, ovoid-shaped vase, 8½ in. high.

COMMENTARY: This pattern, as can be seen, consists of two main sprays along with a range of subsidiary sprays, and is found only on these ovoid vases. As a rule, it is poorly printed and most pieces are heavily blurred. No evidence of the pattern was found in the excavations, but the shape of the vase is known at Worcester and wasters of it in undecorated biscuit were uncovered at the factory site.

DATE RANGE: 1770–1775

RARITY: Uncommon

BORDER NOS: None

MARKS: Hatched crescent, if any.

SHAPES USED: Thrown and turned, baluster-shaped vases, 15 in. high.

COMMENTARY: Although the pattern is named after the design which includes the bunch of rose sprays, the other pattern on the reverse of the vase illustrated apparently only occurs with the principal decoration and never independently. The subsidiary sprays around the shoulders of the vases link this design to 'The Pine Cone Group' (Pattern II.C.11).

Left: *Vase, 15 in. high (Dyson Perrins Museum)*

Right: *Vase Reverse pattern*

Jug, 10 in. high
(Dyson Perrins Museum)

Right: *Jug*
Front pattern

◄ *Jug*
Reverse pattern

DATE RANGE: 1770–1775

RARITY: Not uncommon

BORDER NOS: None

MARKS: Hatched crescent

SHAPES USED: Press-moulded, cabbage-leaf mask jugs, usually 10 in. high.

COMMENTARY: There are three main sprays included in this pattern, always found together on these mask jugs. Each of them has an imaginative quality quite unlike the botanical accuracy of patterns like 'The Passion Flower Sprays' (Pattern II.C.8). Examples can be seen at the Victoria and Albert Museum and the Godden Reference Collection. Caughley used a very similar print, which was illustrated by Godden (Plates 46 and 153).

The Three Flowers

DATE RANGE: 1770–1780

RARITY: Common

BORDER NOS: 2, 32 and F

MARKS: Hatched crescent, sometimes with added letters.

SHAPES USED: A very wide range of thrown and turned as well as press-moulded shapes, including teawares, spittoons, tureens and stands, chocolate cups and stands and butter tubs and stands.

COMMENTARY: This extremely popular floral pattern is characterized by its primary 'three flower' motif which remains consistent regardless of the shape on which it appears. It is possible that this pattern was derived from the subsidiary sprays used in the earlier 'Rose-Centred Spray Group' (Pattern II.C.10). The milk jug illustrated shows a very rare reverse print which can infrequently be found with the principal design. Both Caughley and Lowestoft used this pattern, but the latter was of much poorer quality and can be easily recognized. Biscuit fragments decorated with the design were found at several levels of the excavations on the original factory site, and complete examples are included within most of the major public collections.

Buttertub Stand, 4¾ in. diameter
(Dyson Perrins Museum)

Milk jug and Cover, 5 in. high
Reverse pattern
(Gilbert Bradley Collection)

*Coffee Pot and Cover, 9 in. high
(Godden of Worthing Ltd)*

DATE RANGE: *c.* 1770

RARITY: Rare

BORDER NOS: 1

MARKS: Hatched crescent

SHAPES USED: Plain, thrown and turned coffee or chocolate pots and covers with unusual slender spouts, in a range of sizes up to 9 in. high.

COMMENTARY: This is a somewhat formal style of printed rose pattern, not far removed from those used in painted designs. As far as we know, it was only used on these fairly unusually shaped coffee and chocolate pots. We know of no examples in public collections of porcelain.

Shell Dish, 5¼ in. diameter (Phillips)

DATE RANGE: 1765–1770

RARITY: Not uncommon

BORDER NOS: 4 and 35

MARKS: Hatched crescent

SHAPES USED: Press-moulded as well as thrown and turned shapes, including a variety of tureens, shell-shaped sweetmeat dishes like that illustrated, and as the interior design on chamberpots.

COMMENTARY: The pattern was adapted from a design appearing in *The Ladies' Amusement*, and is usually not found on its own, but rather at the bottom of objects decorated with other printed floral designs such as 'The Rose-Centred Spray Group' (Pattern II.C.10). The shell-shaped dish illustrated was sold by Phillips in its sale of 30 January 1980. A chamber pot with an interior decorated with the pattern can be seen at the Dyson Perrins Museum.

Shell-Shaped Dish, 7⅞ in. diameter
(Authors' Collections)

DATE RANGE: 1770–1785

RARITY: Common

BORDER NOS: 1 or 4

MARKS: Hatched crescent or script 'W'.

SHAPES USED: A very wide range of both thrown and turned and press-moulded shapes other than teawares, but including cylinder and bell-shaped mugs, mask jugs, a range of dessert-wares, pierced baskets, leaf dishes, etc.

COMMENTARY: This is the transfer-printed version of 'The Gilliflower' painted pattern which, in turn, was derived from original designs of the Continental manufacturers, primarily Chantilly. The pattern was quite popular among the English makers and versions were made by Caughley, Pennington's Liverpool, Derby, Caughley-Coalport and Lowestoft, some of which have a very similar appearance to the Worcester design.

*Plate, 8¼ in. diameter
(Dyson Perrins Museum)*

DATE RANGE: *c.* 1775

RARITY: Rare

BORDER NOS: 4

MARKS: Hatched crescent

SHAPES USED: A press-moulded, gadroon-edged plate, 8¼ in. diameter.

COMMENTARY: The central carnation used here appears to be a refined version of the flower in 'The Gilliflower Print' (Pattern II.C.22) preceding, but the other sprays used are unique to this pattern.

*Patty Pan, 5¼ in. diameter
(Godden of Worthing Ltd)*

DATE RANGE: *c.* 1770

RARITY: Very rare

BORDER NOS: None

MARKS: Hatched crescent

SHAPES USED: A plain patty pan, 5¼ in. diameter.

COMMENTARY: This most unusual design apparently is found only on this type of patty pan. The ribbon sprays along the border have some link to similar sprays found on pieces of 'The Pine Cone Group' (Pattern II.C.11), but are basically unique to this pattern. The illustrated example was formerly owned by Godden of Worthing Ltd and Godden illustrates the design in his Caughley-Worcester book (Plate 298).

Teapot and Cover, 5⅜ in. high
(Authors' Collections)

Teapot and Cover
Reverse pattern

DATE RANGE: 1770–1780

RARITY: Common

BORDER NOS: 1 or 7

MARKS: Hatched crescent

SHAPES USED: A wide range of thrown and turned and press-moulded shapes, including teawares, dessertwares, mugs, jugs, and bowls of various sizes.

COMMENTARY: This pattern, which has a stylistic connection with the painted 'Fruit Sprays' (Pattern I.E.14) consists of two designs, the reverse 'sliced fruit' arrangement only being used as a decoration on teapots and apparently on no other shapes. Pieces are often found with a 'rouge de fer' band, but are rarely gilded. Biscuit fragments of the pattern were found in the excavations, and many of the leading public collections will have completed examples. Caughley used this pattern also (see Godden, Plates 123 and 208) in a print almost indistinguishable from the Worcester version, and Pennington's in Liverpool made a very inferior copy as well. The knop on the teapot illustrated has been replaced.

The Marrow and Flower Sprays

DATE RANGE: 1775–1785

RARITY: Uncommon

BORDER NOS: 1

MARKS: Hatched crescent

SHAPES USED: Both thrown and turned and press-moulded shapes, including cabbage-leaf mask jugs of various sizes, cylinder mugs, and fluted shapes of teawares such as teabowls, saucers, and wastebowls similar to that illustrated.

COMMENTARY: This pattern is sometimes used in conjunction with 'The Fruit Sprigs' (Pattern II.C.25) on larger shapes other than teapots (where the 'sliced fruit' motif is usually found), but is also found on its own in a range of teawares. Both biscuit and glost fragments of the pattern were found in the excavations at the factory site wastepits. Godden also illustrates the mask jug (Plate 279).

Top: *Jug, $7\frac{1}{2}$ in. high (Godden of Worthing Ltd)*

Right: *Bowl, $4\frac{1}{2}$ in. diameter Reverse pattern (Private Collection)*

The Fruit and Wreath

Sucrier and Cover, 4⅝ in. high
(Authors' Collections)

DATE RANGE: 1775–1785

RARITY: Not uncommon

BORDER NOS: B

MARKS: Hatched crescent or disguised numerals

SHAPES USED: Both plain thrown and turned and press-moulded tearwares of the usual range.

COMMENTARY: The name of the pattern is taken from that given in the Chamberlain company records, which were probably referring to the similar Caughley version (see Godden, Plate 43). Both biscuit and glost wasters were uncovered in the factory excavations. Godden shows examples of the Worcester pattern (Plates 268 and 299), and other pieces can be seen at the Dyson Perrins and Victoria and Albert Museums.

The Pickle Leaf Fruit

DATE RANGE: 1780–1785

RARITY: Uncommon

BORDER NOS: F

MARKS: Disguised numerals

SHAPES USED: Press-moulded leaf trays, usually $3\frac{1}{2}$ in. by $3\frac{7}{8}$ in.

COMMENTARY: The great difficulty in applying a printed border to an irregular shape such as this often results in an overlapping of the transfer tissue in several places, as can be seen in the leaf tray illustrated. This shape is much more often seen in the painted designs, such as 'The Pickle Leaf Vine' (Pattern I.E.42) or similar patterns. Godden illustrates a leaf tray very much like the one shown here (Plate 285), and other examples can be found at the Dyson Perrins Museum and in the Godden Reference Collection in Worthing.

Leaf Tray, $3\frac{7}{8}$ in. diameter
(Authors' Collections)

III. The Border Patterns

The Painted Borders

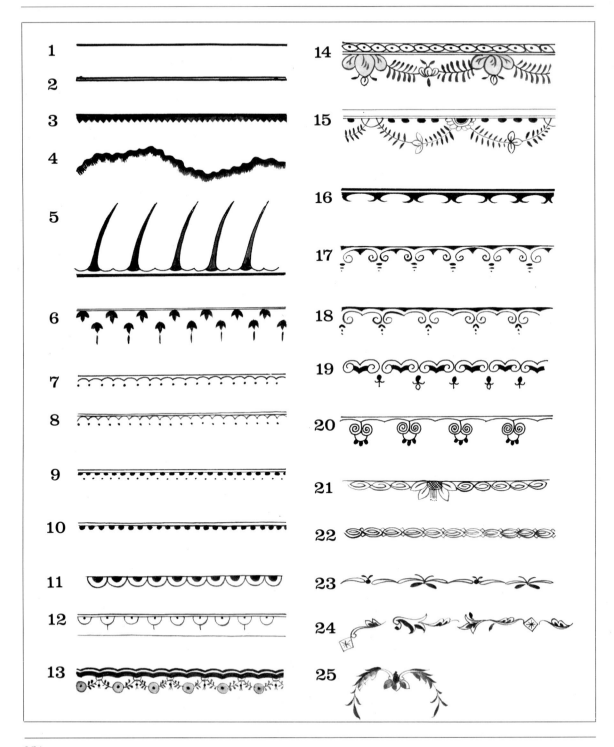

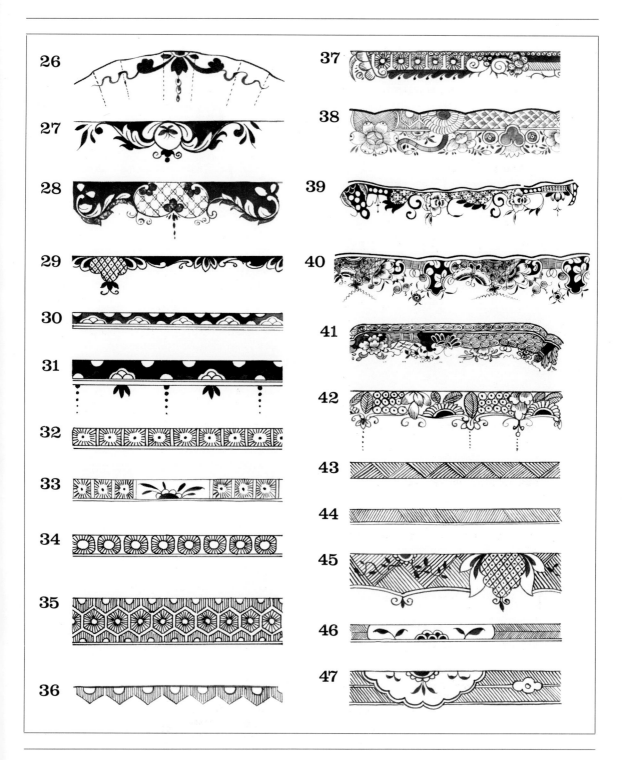

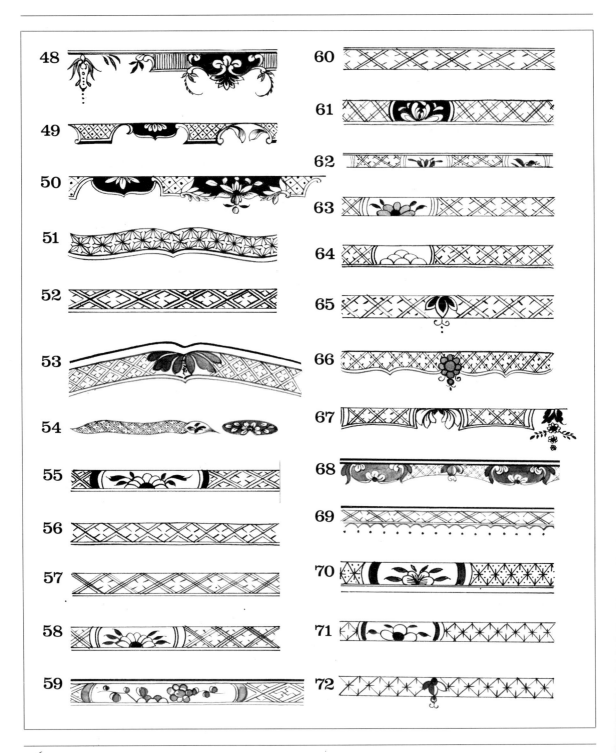

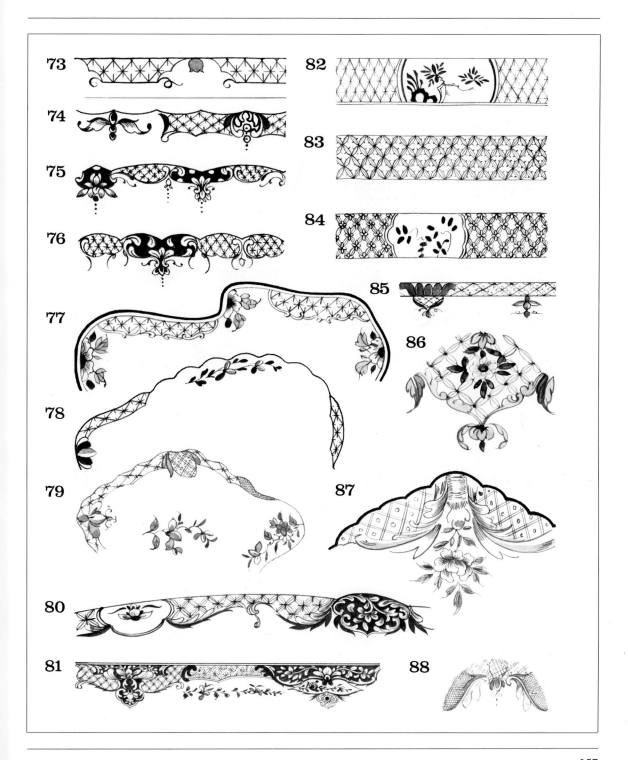

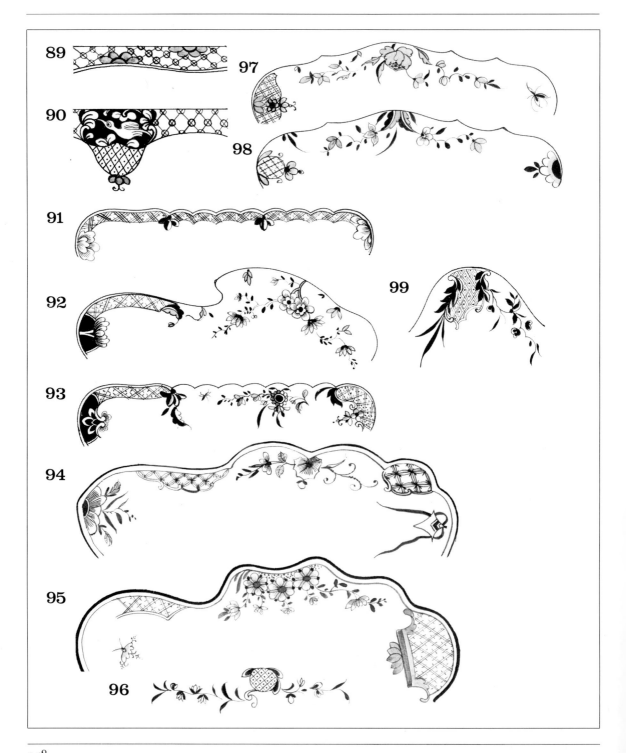

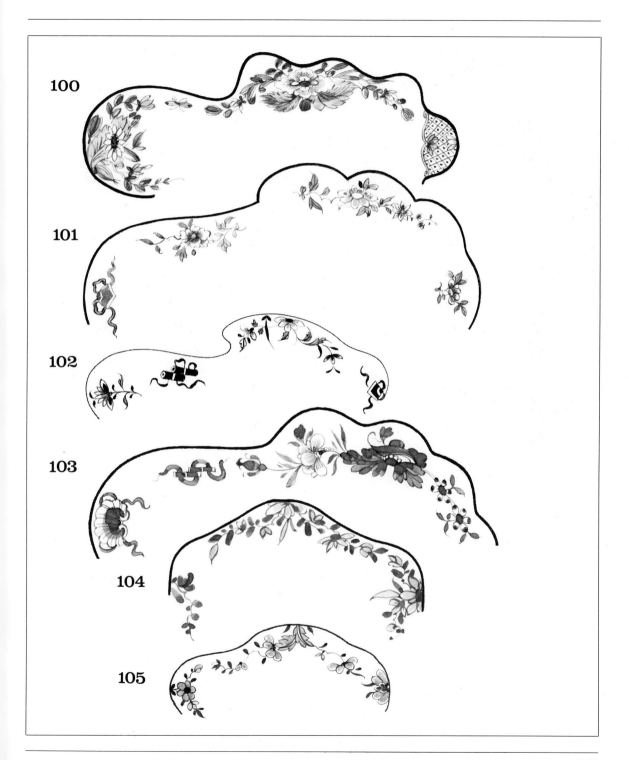

100

101

102

103

104

105

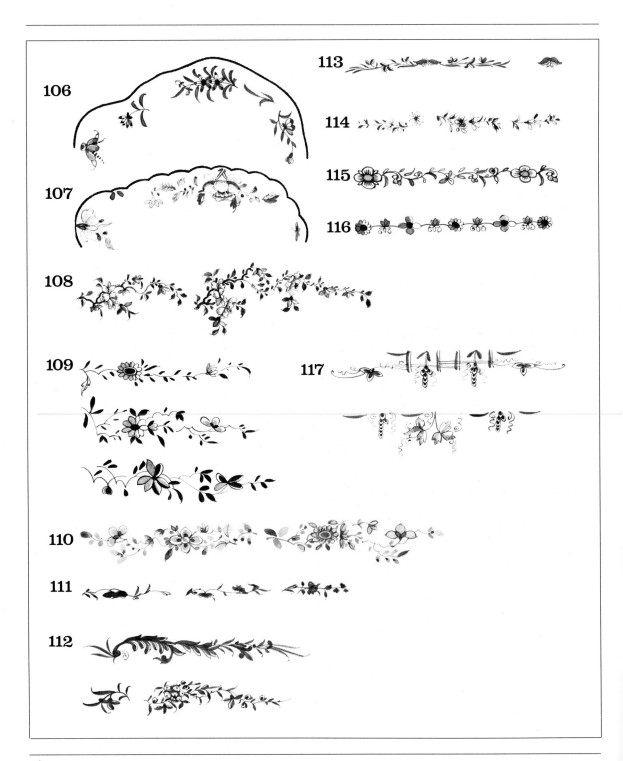

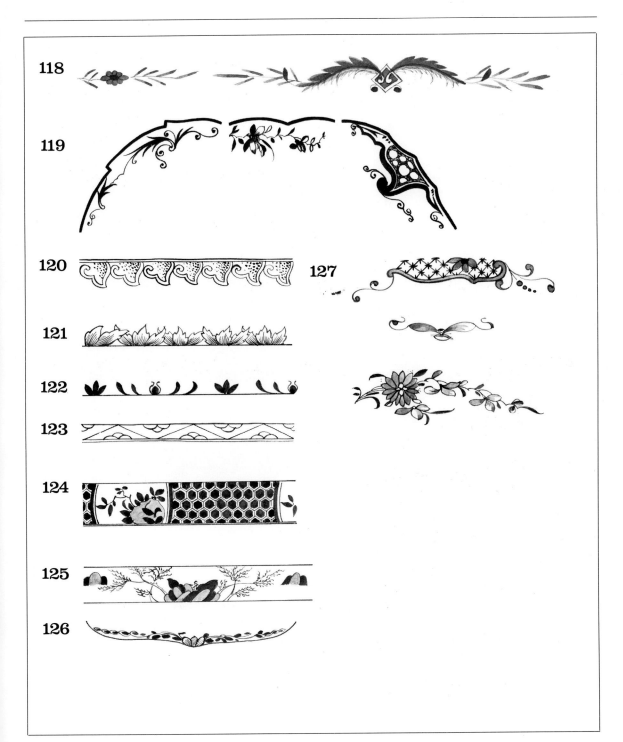

118

119

120

121

122

123

124

125

126

127

The Printed Borders

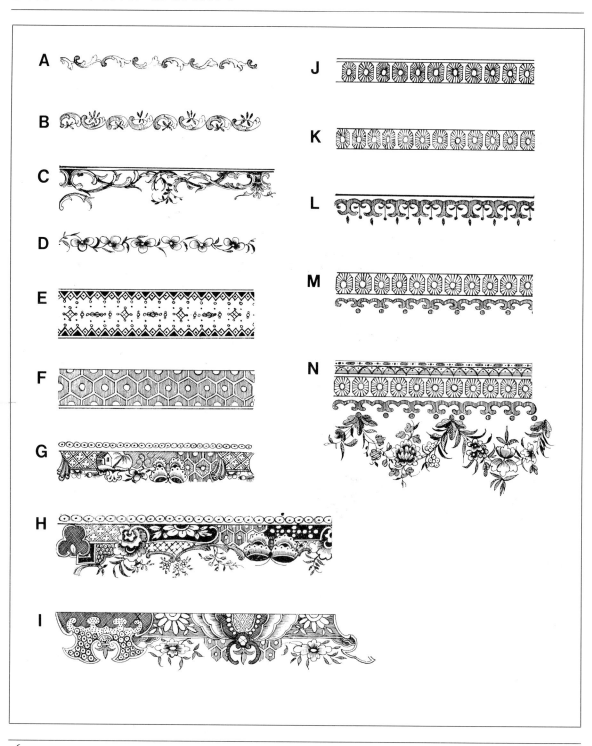

O

P

Q

R

S

T

U

Bibliography

There are nine reference works which we have cited repeatedly throughout this book by the surnames of the authors, as follows:

BARRETT, Franklin A., *Worcester Porcelain and Lund's Bristol*, 2nd edition, Faber and Faber, 1966.

COOK, Cyril, *The Life and Work of Robert Hancock*, Chapman & Hall, 1948, and *Supplement*, 1955.

GODDEN, Geoffrey A., *Caughley and Worcester Porcelains, 1775–1800*, Herbert Jenkins, 1969.

HOBSON, R. L., *Worcester Porcelain*, Bernard Quaritch, 1910.

MACKENNA, F. Severne, *Worcester Porcelain – The Wall Period and its Antecedents*, F. Lewis Publishers, 1950.

MARSHALL, H. Rissik, *Coloured Worcester Porcelain of the First Period*, Ceramic Book Company, 1954.

SANDON, Henry, *The Illustrated Guide to Worcester Porcelain*, 2nd edition, Barrie and Jenkins, 1974 (3rd edition now available).

SPERO, Simon, *The Price Guide to Eighteenth Century English Porcelain*, Antique Collectors' Club, 1970.

WATNEY, Bernard, *English Blue and White Porcelain of the Eighteenth Century*, 2nd edition, Faber and Faber, 1966.

Unfortunately, only the Sandon, Spero and Watney books are still available at booksellers as of this writing, but the others can be found from time to time, either through the auction houses or dealers specializing in out of print books. If you do not own the three reference works which are still in the shops, we would certainly recommend that you acquire them as they are essential to any complete understanding of eighteenth-century English porcelains, and each has made a substantial contribution to our own efforts in preparing this book on the blue and white wares of that period.

Additionally, there are a number of other books which we would recommend as background reading to acquire a better understanding of the porcelain industry and its products during the 1750–1800 period. These are:

AMOR, Albert, Ltd, catalogue to exhibition, *Blue and White 18th Century English Soft Paste Porcelain*, 1979.

BARRETT, Franklin A., *Caughley and Coalport Porcelain*, F. Lewis Publishers, 1951.

BARRETT, Franklin A., and THORPE, Arthur L., *Derby Porcelain*, Faber and Faber, 1971.

BINNS, R. W., *A Century of Potting in the City of Worcester*, Bernard Quaritch, 1878.

BINNS, W. M., *The First Century of English Porcelain*, Bernard Quaritch, 1909.

GARNER, Sir Harry, *Oriental Blue and White*, 5th edition, Faber and Faber, 1977.

GODDEN, Geoffrey A., *The Illustrated Guide to Lowestoft Porcelain*, Herbert Jenkins Ltd, 1969.

GODDEN, Geoffrey A., *Coalport and Coalbrookdale Porcelains*, Herbert Jenkins, 1970.

GODDEN, Geoffrey A., *An Illustrated Encyclopaedia of British Pottery and Porcelain*, 2nd edition, Barrie and Jenkins, 1980.

GODDEN, Geoffrey A., *An Introduction to English Blue and White Porcelains*, privately published, 1974.

GODDEN, Geoffrey A., *British Porcelain – An Illustrated Guide*, Barrie and Jenkins, 1974

GODDEN, Geoffrey A., *Oriental Export Market Porcelain*, Granada Publishing, 1979.

GODDEN, Geoffrey A., *Chamberlain-Worcester Porcelain*, Barrie and Jenkins, 1982.

MACINTOSH, Duncan, *Chinese Blue and White Porcelain*, David and Charles, 1977.

SANDON, Henry, *Flight and Barr Worcester Porcelain 1783–1840*, Antique Collectors' Club, 1978.

Index of Patterns